PUBLISHER'S INTRODUCTION

Dear Readers,

The book you are holding contains more than just a variety of recipes on how to cook good and tasty food, even though it represents the best of Croatian tradition in the skill and culture of food preparation. The wish of the authors is to present Croatia in its many and diverse aspects. *Croatia at Table* offers not only information on the rich and versatile Croatian gastronomic culture, but also many other elements that accompany the country's cuisine. Therefore, it includes the diversity of the Croatian regions, their history and thousand-year-old cultural heritage all of which played a part in the creation of Croatian identity. It tells us of the famous Croats who have devoted themselves and their creative spark at various times over the past thirteen centuries in the effort to preserve and make well-known the name of the Croats, their language and people, despite all obstacles, unfavourable times and foreign incursions, and to found, strengthen and defend the independent and democratic Croatian State.

Croatian dishes are based on the produce of the soil in Croatia: the yield of the continental as well as the Mediterranean areas. The many differences can be seen at Croatia's table.

The dishes described have been chosen with great care. They represent a unique anthology of instructions and suggestions on how to adapt a long tradition in the cuisine of one of the oldest European peoples to the sensibility of modern man, whether from Croatia or abroad - and how to use all the attainments of the modern food processing industry.

The book *Croatia at Table* has been created by a team of authors who have long years of experience in culinary research. Therefore, each dish tells its own different story, not forgetting toasts and information on the best Croatian wines. Without them, Croatia's culinary culture at table would be incomplete, deprived of the joy of dining together. Pleasant dining does not depend solely on tasty food and good wine.

The real pleasure, together with the food and drink, comes from the company, and dining with family members and friends, at various festivities; in other words, at all occasions when people come together in order to enjoy the rich fruits of the soil.

Bon appetit, no matter what dish you chose! And cheers, whichever Croatian wine you enjoy!

I n their anthem, Croats glorify their country for its exceptional beauty: "Our beautiful homeland!" As the poet Drago Ivanišević says in his verses, Croatia is not only the soil, rock, water, clouds and the sea; "Croatia is the tongue I learned from my mother and that which in words is much deeper than words; and that which is deeper ties me to Croatia, with the Croatia of the Croats, with their sufferings, laughter and hope, which binds me to the people, and I as a Croat am brother to all. And wherever I go, Croatia is with me!"

Istrian landscape

Croatia is truly exceptional in its natural beauties and diversity, but also in its thousand-year-old cultural heritage, and in the specific nature of its geographical position constantly at the crossroads of different worlds and cultures. It is a country of Mediterranean characteristics, where the harmony of nature and the talent of its people are accentuated in a very special way; a country belonging to central Europe, always defending the attainments and values

Detail of the Roman Amphitheatre in Pula

of western European

CROATIA AT TABLE

THE AROMAS AND TASTES OF CROATIAN CUISINE

copyright© 1996

by

Ivanka Biluš

Božica Brkan

Lidija Ćorić

Cirila Rodè

PUBLISHERS:
ALFA d.d. Nova Ves 23a Zagreb
PODRAVKA d.d. Koprivnica

FOR THE PUBLISHERS:
Miro Petric
Zvonko Pavlek

CHIEF EDITOR:
Božidar Petrač

EDITORS:
Ivanka Biluš
Zvonimir Mršić

ENGLISH TRANSLATION:
Dunja Knebl
Nina H. Antoljak

LANGUAGE EDITING:
Nina H. Antoljak

ARRANGEMENTS:
Irena Kuzmić
Gordana Maričić

FOOD PREPARATION, CONSULTANTS:
Stanko Erceg
Eleonora Rakeće
Ljiljana Šprem
Marija Bobuš
Nevenka Šavora
Karmen Išek
Ana Čović

FOOD PHOTOGRAPHY:
Davor Marjanović

OTHER PHOTOGRAPHY:
Selection and Consultancy
Ivica Vidović
Photography by:
Ivo Pervan
Tanocki
Slobodan Tadić
Marin Topić
Dragutin Antinac
Damil Kalogjera

DESIGN:
Studio "Piktogram"

PRINTING:
Tiskara "Meić" d.o.o.

Ivanka Biluš, Božica Brkan, Lidija Ćorić,
Cirila Rodè

CROATIA AT TABLE

THE AROMAS AND TASTES OF CROATIAN CUISINE

Zagreb
2003

CIP - Cataloguing in Publication Data of
the National and University Library, Zagreb

UDK 641.568 (497.5)

HRVATSKA za stolom / Ivanka Biluš ... et.
al. - Zagreb: Alfa; Koprivnica: Podravka,
1996. - 192 str. : ilustr. u bojama; 28 cm -
(Biblioteka Anima Croatarum; 2)

Index

ISBN 953-168-104-X

1. Biluš, Ivanka

961 205097

civilisation, the antique Roman and the western Christian. In olden times it was said of individual parts of Croatia: when God created the world, this is how He imagined it. The blueness and the transparency of the sea, the rugged brown mountain heights, the waterfalls of Plitvice Lakes and the Krka River, the hills and slopes of Zagorje and Medimurje, the red soil of Istria and the black soil of Baranja, the golden fields of Slavonia, the aromas of the conifers in the mountains of Gorski Kotar, the whiteness of the Croatian sea-side towns, all the way down south to Dubrovnik - the "Croatian Athens". Croatia is not a large country but nature has lavishly endowed it. Visitors find it hard to forget Croatia, as its beauty is retained by all the senses. Every part of Croatia has its distinctive characteristics, every part is beautiful in its own way. And, of course, through the centuries the Croat generations have added to what nature gave them with their labour and their art. They have defended their country against invaders - in the past and in more recent times.

It is not by chance that the great Dante included in his Divine Comedy the Croatian pilgrim coming to Rome from Croatia to admire "Veronica ours" the real picture, the picture of Christ"; Croatia was not unknown to Shakespeare, to London, to Byron, to Joyce, to Eleonora Duse, and Isadora Duncan, nor to the great 19th century classical Russian writers. Rightly so, because the treasury of culture and natural beauty in Croatia is difficult to surpass and not easy to forget. Proud of its past, Croatia also looks to the future.

J a b u k a   I s l a n d

WHO ARE THE CROATS?

The ethno-genesis of the Croatian people has not yet been explained in full, and there are a number of theories on where they came from before moving into the regions which were to become their homeland. It is, however, known that the name "Croat(s)" referred to the people who had founded their community between Nin and Cetina in Dalmatia. At the crossroads of East and West, the Croatian people converted to the Christian faith, gaining the first marks of their state independence and sovereignty from the pontiff of Rome, Pope Agathon (678-681), with whom an agreement was signed pledging that the Croats would never attack other lands. The first trace of the Croatian name is found in the diplomatic documents of Prince Trpimir dated March 4, 852 where he is named as "dux Chroatorum iuvatus munere divino", and the country as "regnum Chroatarum". During the reign of Prince Branimir (879 - 892), who wisely depended on Pope John VIII for support against incursions by the Franks and Byzantium, Croatia became a completely independent land. When the Croatian Prince Tomislav came to the throne, Croatia was proclaimed a kingdom in 925, and he was given the title of Croatia's king (rex Chroatorum) in papal documents. This is how the mediaeval Croatian country grew from the middle of the 7th century to become a completely independent principality at the end of the 9th century, and, as early as the first half of the 10th century it became an independent kingdom governed by a national dynasty till the end of the 11th century.

Church of the Holy Cross in Nin - Detail

THE CROATIAN LANGUAGE

The Croats speak and write Croatian, which belongs to the Slavic languages group. It consists of three dialects, Kajkavian, Čakavian and Štokavian. Croatian is also spoken in countries which are the ethnic and historical home of Croats today (Bosnia, Herzegovina, Vojvodina, and coastal Montenegro), and quite a lot in countries and regions to which Croats emigrated a long time ago (Burgenland in Austria, Hungary, Romania, Slovakia, the Molise district in Italy, and in Kosovo). The Kajkavian dialect is spoken in the Hrvatsko Zagorje and Gorski Kotar regions of Croatia; Čakavian is spoken in Istria, the northern part of the Croatian Littoral, on the islands, in north-western Lika and throughout Dalmatia. Štokavian is spoken in the remaining parts of Croatia. Today the Štokavian dialect is the foundation for Croatian literary standards, and is used by the Kajakvians and the Čakavians. But the Croatian standard literary language is not void of

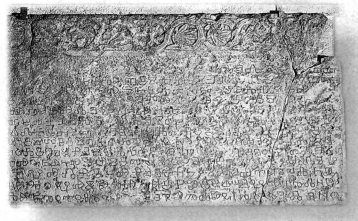

The Baška Inscription Stone (around 1100)

Čakavian and Kajkavian forms. The Croats have used three scripts during their thirteen-century history : the Glagolitic script, the Croatian version of the Cyrillic alphabet (Bosančica) and the Latin alphabet. During the Ottoman invasions a new component of the Croatian written culture was formed: texts in Croatian, written in the Bosnian Arabic script. The specific national script - the Glagolitic script - was the script used in all the first Croatian stone inscriptions. This Glagolitic script was used exclusively by the Croats. Similarly to other peoples, on their way to a common vernacular the Croats did not exclude the dialects, but adapted and united them - and the Croats too - in the Croatian literary language. The Croatian writer Antun Gustav Matoš said the following in describing the Croatian language: "Only our beautiful homeland could have created the beauty of our wonderful language, the marvellous words as beautiful as islands, beautiful gardens floating in the sea".

EDUCATION, SCIENCE AND CULTURE

By their acceptance of Christianity in the 7th century, the Croatian people living in the historical areas of Croatia, Slavonija, Istria and Dalmatia, Bosnia, Dubrovnik and Boka Kotorska became part of the western European civilisation and have remained so for more than 13 centuries.

Bela Csikos - Sessia, Baptism of the Croats

the Croats as their Glagolitic alphabet. Juraj of Slavonia, a student at the Sorbonne and, later, professor at the University of Paris informed his Parisian colleagues about the "Croatian bishop who, knowing both Latin and Croatian, performed the liturgy in both languages, constantly alternating them".

Christianity has left a deep mark in the spirituality, moral outlook and culture of the Croats, and the Croatian heritage, both oral and written. The Croats are the only people of the western Christian body who have maintained a thousand-year liturgical tradition in the vernacular. The script created by the Ćiril and Metodius, Apostles of the Slavs, was accepted by

He also told them that the Glagolitic script (he called it the Croatian alphabet) was used by the "clergy of Istria, which is part of our homeland, and the bishops of Krbava, Knin, Krk, Split, Trogir, Šibenik, Zadar, Nin, Rab, Osor and Senj".

The fragments of a beam bearing the name of Prince Branimir found in Muć near Split, the gable with the

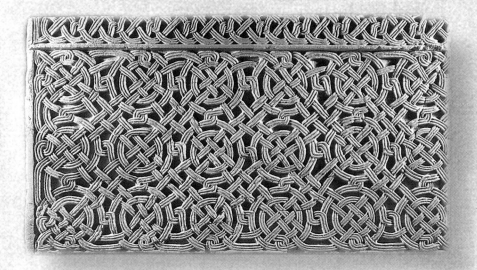

tional language and script (Glagolitic) being in official use. Today the Stone is kept in the Croatian Academy of Arts and Sciences in Zagreb. Herman Dalmatin from Istria founded Croatian science in the 12th century, and was one of the European pioneers in this field of human knowledge. He wrote some twenty independent literary works, compilations and translations on the subjects of astronomy, philosophy, and mathematics, incorporating the learning of antiquity, and elements of Indian, Chaldean, Assyrian and Arabic wisdom.

name of Prince Trpimir discovered at Rižinac near Solin, and many other similarly preserved stone fragments and plates, as well as numerous Glagolitic manuscripts provide evidence on how the very first rulers nurtured literacy, science and art. Prince Trpimir first invited the Benedictines to his land to teach the people to read and write, the Cistercian order followed and it is thanks to their efforts that spiritual and material culture developed, especially written works of art, and the Romanesque and Gothic architecture. The oldest Croatian monument with writing, a stone inscription written in Croatian Glagolitic script, is the Baška Inscription Stone (1100) from the island of Krk. This is not only political, but also artistic and philosophical evidence on the existence of a Croatian na-

Korčula Cathedral - Detail

The announcement by the 3rd Lateran parliament (1179) that "the poor also have the right to the wealth of the spirit" led the Zagreb bishop Augustin Kažotić to organize a higher level of studies, "artes" (free skills) and theology.

There are other Croatians who need to be mentioned: Pavao Dalmatinac, the esteemed professor at the Bologne University and organiser of the Croatian Dominican province, Ivan Stojković, Matija Vlačić Ilirik, Franjo Petrić, Faust Vrančić and, especially Ruđer Bošković, the world famous scientist. The first institutions of higher learning "studia generalia" - were founded in the Croatian area in the 15th, 16th, and 17th centuries, with university privileges granted to the Dominicans in Zadar (1493), the Jesuits in Zagreb (1669) and the Paulines at Lepoglava (1671). Dubrovnik also becomes an important significant Jesuit centre, where Bartol Kašić not only wrote the first Croatian grammar, but translated the Bible in its entirety. In 1607 he

Šibenik Cathedral - Detail

organised in Zagreb the first humanistic grammar school in this part of Europe.

Immediately after Guttenberg invented the printing press Croats became very interested in printing books. The first Croatian and South Slav printed book, a Missal, was soon completed, on February 22, 1483. This was the peak of Croatian Glagolitic activity, a splendid conclusion to the Middle Ages in Croatia. This masterpiece of printing skill had been anticipated by the Missal of Prince Novak dating from 1386, written in the prince's own hand. In the last pages of the Missal Juri Žakan from Roč wrote the following proud and enthusiastic words: "Vita, Vita! Our printing is developing!" The first Croatian printing house was founded in Senj, which produced a beautiful Missal, also written in Glagolitic script in 1494.

The Croatian Latinists opened an independent chapter of the European civilisation, joining the great humanism movement spreading throughout cultural Europe in the 14th century. Ilija Crijević from Dubrovnik was crowned with a poet's wreath in Rome as one of the most important literary artists writing in Latin. Marko Marulić of Split holds a similar position in Croatian literature and culture, to that of the great Florentine, Dante, in Italy, a writer of world fame. Marulić used both Croatian and Latin with equal skill, and his works in Latin were best-sellers of those times in Europe, translated into many European languages, in multiple editions. Just as the beginning of the Middle Ages in literature is symbolised by the Baška Inscription Stone, Judita by Marko Marulić is the first book printed in Croatian verse. It was published in Venice in 1521, and symbolised the beginning of a new era developed on the foundation of ecclesiastic literary tradition and folk poetry, respecting the folk tradition, early Croatian religious poetry, Latin, and Petrarchian Renaissance tradition. The playwright Marin Držić (1508 - 1567), evaluated as unsurpassed in Croatian literature - a predecessor of both the great Shakespeare and Molière - is a very famous name in Croatian and European comediography.

If culture is what remains when everything

Šibenik Cathedral Dome

else is destroyed, there could be endless examples in the great Croatian literary mosaic, up until modern times. Literature for children has its great names too, its first lady being Ivana Brlić - Mažuranić. Finally, books were an anthology of the Croatian tragedy from 1990 to 1995. During that time, translated into many languages, Croats used words to protect and shield their country and their European cultural identity. As to the visual arts, real gems may be found in any part of Croatia you visit. Together with the famous Croatian interlace pattern, the special Višeslav Baptistery near the town of Nin dates from the early period of the Croatian state - although not much is known about it - and with its form and Latin inscription testifies the entry by the Croats into a new, lit-

erate civilisation. Among architectural treasures are a group of old Croatian churches of unique beauty which have forms unknown to any European peoples from such early times.

Romanesque cathedrals, palaces and monasteries were built in the Middle Ages proper in the towns of Trogir, Zadar, Rab and Krk, while the Gothic style can be seen in Zagreb Cathedral and a number of big monasteries built by the Pauline and Dominican orders, and the Franciscans (in Dubrovnik, Zagreb, and Lepoglava). Istrian churches are in the Gothic style, with exceptionally beautiful frescoes in the St. Mary's church in Berm. The greatest Croatian Renaissance sculptor, Juraj Dalmatinac, carved realistic portraits of his contemporaries on the

I. Meštrović, The History of the Croats

N. Božidarević, St. Blaise Holding Dubrovnik

external side of the Šibenik Cathedral apse. Nikola Božidarević is a famous painter from Dubrovnik who lived and worked in that period. Julije Klović (Clovio), was considered the greatest miniaturist of his times and proudly stressed that he was a Croat. Andrija Medulić is yet another famous late Renaissance painter.

The northern parts of Croatia are particularly marked by Baroque works of art. But so is Dubrovnik. More recent times brought new approaches and new ideas following the general trends in art, but not without the recognisable expression of painters like Bukovac and Medović, Kraljević and Becić, Babić and Herman, Job and Plančić. Krsto Hegedušić founded the Hlebine school of Croatian primitive art in 1930, its most famous artists being Ivan Generalić and Mirko Virius. After World War II came Miljenko Stančić, Ivo Dulčić and Josip Vaništa, Edo Murtić, the initiator of Croatian abstract painting, and Ivan Rabuzin, Ivan Lacković Croata and Dino Botteri. The style of photographer/artist Zvonimir Mihanović is distinctive. The continuity in distinctive sculpture has never been

T h e   B e l l - T o w e r s   o f   R a b

broken since the works of Ivan Rendić, Robert Fran- geš Mihanović, with the role and position of Ivan Meš- trović, a world fam- ous sculptor, be- ing very special. There have been many other fam- ous names in other fields or art, such as music and the theatre. The Zagreb School of Animated Film attracted world-wide attention. Croa- tian culture, the fruitful crossroads of four cultural influences - western, east- ern, north central European and south Mediterranean - is the foundation for works of art which have enriched the European, and, in some cas- es, world culture and art as

The BP Jazz Club in Zagreb

Zagreb

well. In other words, the Croatian spiritual identity is distinguishable as a part of the European spiritual entity. Today in a new era, the era of national emanci- pation, at the end of the 20th century and at the begin- ning of a new mil- lennium, all the necessary conditions and foundations are in place for full development. Croatian sports results speak for themselves.

If the past was almost out of reach to us as a people, times have changed and we can build our everyday life and the present with hope that the future is already dwelling in Croatia.

THIRTEEN CENTURIES OF THE CROATIAN NATION

The entire political and cultural life of the Croats unfolded in the Croatian lands, Slavonia, Dalmatia, Bosnia and Dubrovnik with Boka Kotorska; these represent the historical regions of the Croatian people. At the time of the early beginnings of the creation of the Croatian state, it encompassed the coastal land beside the Adriatic Sea, from Raša in Istria to the mouth of the Cetina River, and inland as far as Velika Kapela, Grmeč mountain and the Vrbas River south to near the Neretva River. The dividing line was drawn between the Western Roman and Eastern Roman Empires at the end of the 4th century; the Croatians who had their own independent state by the end of the 9th century on the cross-roads between the two, were constantly exposed to various external threats and incursions, and tried to rebuff and overcome them, with considerable difficulty and sacrifice. After the fall of the national sovereigns - King Petar Krešimir IV from 1058-1075, at a time when Croatian borders were at their most extensive, and the death of Dmitar Zvonimir the Just, who, almost inconceivably for his time, wanted to abolish slavery among his subjects - the Croatian kingdom entered into a personal union with the land of the Magyars (the union lasted from 1102 until 1526) and then came under the Hapsburg crown from 1527 until 1918.

C. Medović, The Split Synode in 925

17

Throughout that entire period, the Croats had their own Ban [Governor] and the Croatian parliament remained the standard-bearer of national sovereignty and the defender of Croatian statehood. Complex historical circumstances did, of course, impose defensive wars on the Croats, particularly during the Ottoman invasions between the 15th and 19th centuries. Heads often rolled because of the indifference of the West to calls for assistance in stopping the Ottoman advance. Throughout the almost five centuries of battles with the Ottoman conquerors, when Croatia was reduced to a mere *reliquiae reliquiraum* of the once powerful kingdom with its territory divided between three empires, it still managed to maintain itself both as a historical fact and as a irremovable and indivisible part of the western world, particularly in respect to its scientific, literary and cultural attainments and contributions to European and world civilisation. Because of its geopolitical position, always like a flower at the cross-roads, between East and West, rarely protected other than by its own people, with its troubled historical experience and rare flaring of hope such as the Croatian National Revival in the 19th century, Croatia had to confront the unrelenting events of the

The Belec Baroque Church - Detail

20th century. First came the fall of the Austro-Hungarian monarchy after World War I and, in keeping with the Treaty of Versailles, Croatia's entry into Yugoslavia, within which the Croatian parliament - the Sabor - was left without any say. True enough, the Croatian parliament never did ratify the decision on unification with the Kingdom of Serbia and brought down no decisions relating to the organisation of the new multi-national state. It was not long before Serbian policy showed itself in full, culminating in the shooting of Stjepan Radić, leader of the largest Croatian political party between the wars - the Croatian Peasant Party - and a number of Croatian representatives on the floor of the Assembly in Belgrade on June 20, 1928. In the following year, Aleksandar I of the ruling house of Karađorđević proclaimed the Sixth of January Dictatorship, while the

O. Iveković, Croatian Nobles with the Hungarian King Koloman in 1102.

Croats responded in 1932 with the Zagreb Points Declaration condemning absolutism, Serbian hegemony and the centralist organisation of the state, and set out their demands for equality of the individual elements of the complex state. Circumstances led to Serbian policy becoming somewhat more elastic, and negotiations between Cvetković - on behalf of the Serbs - and Maček - on behalf of the Croats - led to the constitution on August 26, 1939, of the unified Banovina of Croatia. However, this compact was not to enjoy a long life. The Serbs were reluctant to implement those aspects by which the Banovina - with its own Ban or governor - would be entitled to function autonomously. General conditions in Europe, too, were not conducive to the establishment of the Banovina of Croatia. In a complex web of relationships, the outbreak of World War II brought major, new misfortunes. After the fall of Yugoslavia, the NDH - the Independent State of Croatia - was declared on April 10, 1941. This entity was intended to be more than a mere component part of the Axis coalition; it was also meant to meet the yearning of the Croats for formation of their own state independence. But it soon became clear that the price payable for this independence was far too high. Italy annexed the Istrian peninsular, the Croatian Littoral, Dalmatia and the islands; the Croatian government was forced to introduce racist laws and undertake measures emulating the Axis models, particularly Germany and Italy. The armed anti-Fascist uprising began. In those turbulent times, with the ensuing confusion in identification of the armies and objectives of the individual military and political groups - the Chetniks for example - the NDH was soon to disappear forever from the world stage. Croatia became part of the newly created Federal People's Republic of Yugoslavia. The new communist regime was involved at the very

beginning in a number of reprisals against the Croats and in massacres - the Bleiburg tragedy - and in purges and show trials, including that of Cardinal Alojz Stepinac, the Zagreb archbishop. It carried out Bolshevik indoctrination and collectivisation of society. Briefly, the communist system did not manage to settle any issues, and meant new suffering, migration and dissolution of identity for the Croats. The fall of the Berlin Wall and of communism in the countries of central and eastern Europe in 1989/1990 brought a new opportunity. Calling on Starčević's state law and self-determination, the Croats were able to use the elections to achieve their independence and sovereignty. The programme of the Croatian Democratic Union - the HDZ - brought together the majority of Croats, and at the first post-war free elections which were held on April 22 and May 17, 1990, it was the winning party. On May 30, 1990 the multi-party Croatian Sabor was constituted, and the Constitution of the Republic of Croatia was voted in on December 22 of the same

K. Kovačić, Hvar Cathedral Interior

year. Dr Franjo Tuđman was elected president of the Republic of Croatia. Croatia returned to the free western world, and at a referendum held on May 19, 1991 the majority of its citizens voted for full independence and sovereignty. Croatia wanted to join the European community of free nations and states, seeing it as the bridge which would bring together peoples and nations, allowing all individuals and nations to be free and equal. Croatia's vision of the future of Europe has never differed from that of any other country which has chosen democratic values, parliamentary democracy and the rule of law. On June 25, 1991 the Croatian Sabor voted to establish an independent and sovereign Croatian state. Prior to this decision - and after it - there was widespread and organised insurgency in Croatia, which finally grew into open Serbian aggression. During this aggression by supporters of Greater Serbia and by the JNA - the Yugo-

slav People's Army - Croatia fought a war which is unique in the annals of re-

The Đakovo Cathedral Interior

cent European history. Croatia, alone and without help, secured its inalienable rights to freedom and independence. After centuries of life in multi-national states, this just struggle and determination to return to an independent national state community was crowned with international recognition on January 15, 1992, membership in the United Nations Organisation on May 22, 1992, and membership in the Council of Europe on April 24, 1996. The number of victims of the war and the great devastation that it brought throughout the country provide the surety that the Croats will build their future on the foundations and heritage of the humanistic, democratic and free world.

CROATIA - EXPERIENCE IT FOR YOURSELF

The beauty of Croatia - which greets the eye at every step, and has drawn conquerors throughout history - is finally an advantage compounded by the fact of its proximity to the entire world, as a Central European and Mediterranean country. With the expansion of roads and railways during the 19th century, tourism had started to develop. Now you can take your pick of urban and rural tourism, continental and sea-side holidays, cultural tours or Robinson Crusoe solitude on an uninhabited Adriatic island, mountain-climbing or fishing, hunting or sailing. Zagreb is the Croatian metropolis in every sense of the word. It is a modern city with its soul sketched out in the colours on the roof of St Mark's Church and on the Stone Gates which link the nine-century-old history of Gradec, the Upper Town, and Kaptol, with the nineteenth century charms of the Lower Town and the unique Lenuci Horseshoe, a series of cultivated park areas, all in harmony with the modern suburbs growing up in what was the Roman settlement of Andautonia.

The Dubrovnik Fortress Walls

Dubrovnik on the southern Adriatic coast is a world tourism

destination and recognised monument-city, one of the most

significant preserved historical urban entities in Europe, girded

with unusually well-preserved Renaissance ramparts with tow-

ers such as Lovrjenac, Revelin, Minčeta. Particular points of

interest within the walled city include the Regent's Palace, the

Sponza Palace and the harmonious layout of the narrow streets

leading into the Stradun, the main thoroughfare. The city's basic

appearance today dates from the 18th century and it was built

according to a mu-

nicipal building

plan as were Venice

and Amsterdam. The

territory of the for-

mer Dubrovnik Re-

public houses has some eighty intact summer residences built

for the aristocratic families in the 16th century. As early as the

14th century, Dubrovnik's trading and diplomatic activities re-

quired not only the establishment of organised sleeping accom-

modation for visitors but also a quarantine station - the Lazare-

tum - today also one of the city's points of interest.

In 1884, Opatija in the northern Adriatic opened its first hotel,

the Kvarner. In 1902, the dancer Isadora Duncan sang an inspir-

ing song about the palm tree which grew beneath the window

S p l i t   b y   N i g h t

of her room in the Villa Amalia. This was followed by many songs about the enchanting resort, the Old Lady and her camel-

lias. As well as the beauties of its coast-line, the Istrian pe-ninsula boasts the world's smallest town,

H v a r

Hum. It stands on the top of a hill only 277 metres high, reached by as many as 1 252 steps. One should not miss visiting the fairy-tale town of Moto-vun which is linked with legends about Joža the Giant, who was immortalised by the writer Vladimir Nazor.

Building a holiday home beneath Marjan in the 4th century, the Roman emperor Diocletian was unaware that his palace built around the year 300 would lay the foundations for today's Split,

a city which wisely incorporated past times into its modern beauty. The church of St Domnius was originally built as an imperial mausoleum, the baptistery of St John as a Roman temple, the Peristyle ...

The theatre in Hvar is both the first Croatian theatre, and one of the first public buildings erected in Europe, and the town itself grew from the Greek settlement, Dimos, established in the 4th century BC. Grey mullet still breed in the fishpond of the poet Petar Hektorović's summer house park, just as they did many centuries ago. The island of Hvar's mild climate, even during the winter, with the highest average of sunny days annually in Europe, the lilac hues of the flowering fields of lavender as if they had come from the paint-

B r e l a

Modra špilja (Blue Cave)

ings of Celestin, and the experience gained since 1841 when the first island hotel was opened, offer a welcome that is all one could desire. One of the ideal spots on the island of Brač is the Zlatni rat [Golden Cape] beach. All of the islands, from Cres and Lošinj, through Rab and Pag, Korčula and Vis, to the most distant, smallest and isolated lighthouses on Jabuka, Brusnik, Kamnik or Svetac, have their undiscovered beauty spots and secrets. Just as Ulysses did - so the legend says - you can sail around the Adriatic islands, pulling in to the small island of Biševo with its Blue Cave, considered to be one of Croatia's most intriguing natural phenomena. Cres, too, has its natural wonder: the freshwater Vransko Lake. Today a busy traffic crossroads, Karlovac is one of the rare Croatia towns to have been built to

plan. It was established in 1579 at the intersecting point of the three main traffic arteries of the time - the Carolina, Josephina and Louisiana highways - and at the meeting-point of four major rivers. Built in the layout of a six-pointed star, it was an ideally proportioned Renaissance town.

Croatia is an ideal location for all forms of tourism throughout

K   o   r   n   a   t   i

the four seasons of the year. It has much more to offer than its five hundred hotels, some eighty tourist settlements, a few hundred camping areas and fifty or so marinas. Those looking for Robinson Crusoe experiences will avoid the bustle of the cities and choose not to spend time admiring the historical architectural styles and master-craftsmanship. They

P   a   g

will prefer the Kornati archipelago. Writing about those more than one thousand and forty large and small islands and reefs, George Bernard Shaw said: *The gods wanted to crown their labours, so on the last day they created the Kornati from tears, the stars and the breath of the sea.* Seafarers can sail wherever the fair winds takes them along Croatia's indented Adriatic coastline. There are some fifty well-equipped marinas where they can drop anchor.

Croatia is a country which has produced world and Olympic champions in basketball, waterpolo, handball, tennis and table tennis, as well as in boxing and other sports. Attention is given to providing open-air and indoor sports facilities, and on a time-to-time or permanent basis, the country hosts international

sporting events such as the ATP tournament in Umag and the Golden Pirouette skating competition in Zagreb. The mountains are there for climbers, and lovely woods and national parks for hikers and nature enthusiasts. Fishermen and anglers can try their luck with the trout in rivers such as the Mrežnica and the Gacka, which is regarded as one of the most beautiful and purest rivers in the world. There are ornithological reserves at Kopački Rit near Osijek with its unique bird habitat, and at Lonjsko

The River Krka Waterfalls

Polje and Čigoč, famed for its European stork village. Game hunting is a particularly developed tourism segment in Croatia and hunters come from all over Europe to hunt deer, wild boar and marten in the continental hunting grounds; mountain goats in the Dalmatian Zagora region and on Biokovo mountain; and fallow deer on the islands of Cres and Mali Lošinj. Game fowl are found in the surroundings of the towns of Đurđevac, Čakovec, Virovitica, Pula, Jastrebarsko and Zelendvor.

Health tourism is found at the same locations visited by the Romans, who discovered the majority of the continental spas - at Varaždin, Krapina, Stubica, Tuhelj and Daruvar, Topusko and in Istria. Umag, Opatija, Veli Lošinj, Hvar, Makarska, Vela Luka and Crikvenica are famed for their therapeutic air spas, with

a history of more than 150 years of health tourism. Ma-

rija Bistrica, Trsat and Sinj have a century-old tradition of pilgrimages, and the renascence of religious tourism in the last decade is connected with Međugorje in Herzegovina. One can also go skiing in Croatia at the centres in the Croatian Switzerland - Gorski Kotar - at Delnice, Mrkopalj, Bjelolasica and Platak not far from Rijeka, and

Medvednica near Zagreb.

Nature enthusiasts will fall in love with a country which boasts 4,300 plant species, more than 23,000 land animal species, with more than 530 species of fish, cephalopods, crustaceans and shell-fish in the Adriatic. Many of the rivers are protected nature areas. Some 7.5 percent of Croatia's territory represents preserved and protected natural environments. Of the seven national parks, three - Risnjak, Paklenica and Plitvica Lakes - are in mountain regions, and four - the

The Miljana Manor

27

Kornati, Mljet, and Brioni islands and the Krka River - are in the coastal region. Brioni consists of two large and 12 small islands in a preserved natural and cultural setting. The Krka is a beautiful river which winds through karst countryside with a series of waterfalls, the most fascinating being Skradinski Buk. The tiny island of Visovac in the middle of the river is home to a Franciscan monastery, and the antique settlement of Skradin - with its modern marina - stands at its mouth. Mljet is the most densely wooded Adriatic island, and Paklenica on Croatia's highest mountain, Velebit, which is reputed to be home to fairies, is the most popular alpine hiking destination in Croatia. Velebit, along with Cres, hosts one of the last habitats of the Griffon Vulture in Europe. Risnjak got its name from the ris, or lynx, one of the inhabitants of that heavily timbered Gorski Kotar region, part of the mountain

The Plitvice Lakes

range where the vegetation enjoys the advantages of the blending of the coastal and continental climate between the Dinaric mountains and the Alps. This is one of the rare places where one can find - but not pick - the edelweiss flower. The natural beauty of the Plitvice Lakes is breathtaking and the lakes are listed by UNESCO as one of the one hundred items in Humankind's World Heritage. Through an area some ten kilometres long, the sixteen lakes flow one into the other over a series of cascades and waterfalls. Croatia indeed has much to offer its visitors, whatever their interests and tastes may be.

THE ECONOMY

Croatia is an industrial and agricultural country, and production of food, in addition to tourism, is one of the strategic segments of its economy. The fertile soil of the flat Pannonian region, particularly in Baranja and eastern Slavonia, has suf-

ficient water and the necessary mild continental climate to ensure high yields of grain - wheat, barley, oats - industrial plants, fruit and vegetables.

The Dinaric mountain region with its harsh climate and heavy snows, has pine forests and upland pastures, suitable for the rearing of cattle and sheep. Because of its warm Mediterranean climate, the Adriatic region has lots of sunlight but a shortage of water and arable land. Other than parts of Istria, Ravni Kotari in the hinterland of Zadar and the Neretva valley, the land has had to be reclaimed from the stone in the karst areas, and the precious soil protected by the typical dry stone walls. Here olives, vines, figs, carob, and vegetables are grown and the people pick medicinal herbs, collect wild vegetables and fish. The discovery of the New World brought new plants such as tobacco in the 16th century, potatoes in the 17th and sunflowers at the beginning of the 19th. Oil beet was raised by the Romans who used the oil for their lanterns.

Stock rearing is another important activity. Over the last few years horse-breeding has been given renewed attention, particularly breeding of the Posavina horse whose body temperature adapts to and fluctuates with its environment and the Lippizaner breed from the Đakovo stud farm, a beauti-

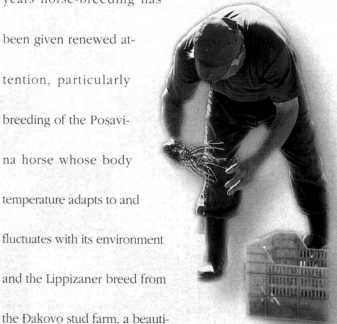

and farming, and recommends that it be replaced by intensive practices.

A curiosity in the animal world are the Istrian cattle, or Boškarin breed, and the autochthonic dogs such as the Croatian sheep dog, the Posavinian pointer, and the Istrian short-haired and long-haired pointers who have developed from

working field dogs. The elegant white dog with black spots - the Dalmatian - wins all hearts with

ful horse which has a long tradition among the Croats. When the Croats moved into the territory which is now their home-land, they brought with them the Tarpan breed from the steppes; Constantine Porfyrongenitus, the emperor-historian, mentioned that the Croats were able to raise a cavalry of 60 000 horsemen in the 10th century. Hog raising was developed in the common oak regions such as Slavonia and Turopolje and the pigs who fed on their acorns were particularly prized. Historians have found written confirmation concerning sheep raising in a 10th century will from Zadar. In the 18th century,

its beauty and good nature. There is also a series of poultry species, including the autochthonic Croatian fowl. Being a tax-exempt

Matija Antun Reljković in his *Satir iliti divji čovjek* [The Satyr or the Wild Man] advocates the abandonment of extensive stock-raising

activity, poultry raising attracted investment and development.

The food processing industries are also well developed: meat-processing, milling and bakery, confectionery, and brewing. These industries are major Croatian exporters placing processed meat, fruit, vegetables and particularly wine on markets abroad. Amalgamating modern technological achievement with sound traditions and persistence, this strate-

gic segment of industrial development has managed to win a leading market share with the quality of its products, in competition with leading world companies. Over the last few years Croatian firms have been using their own original trade marks with great success. For example, the PODRAVKA company from Koprivnica has managed to place world-wide its

products such as Vegeta, and its baby food and packet soups, and has proved itself financially as a worthwhile and reliable partner.

It is interesting to note that apart from ecclesiastical schools, the first Croatian schools, such as the one in Križevci founded in 1860, were agricultural schools. All this contributed to Croatian cuisine, the cuisine of its regions and counties, being tasty and rich in its diversity.

CROATIAN EMIGRANTS

Croatia's geopolitical position was the cause of the first emigrations of the Croats in face of the Ottoman incursions. People living in the insecure southern regions had constantly been on the move to the hinterland of the Croatian Kingdom's northern regions. During that period, the Croats migrated into south-western Hungary and to the western Austrian provinces particularly, Carniola and Styria, and to the Italian province of Molise.

In the mid-nineteenth century, Croatian emigration en masse to distant overseas countries began. Statistical estimates speak of 340 000 persons emigrating by the beginning of World War I, with another 150 000 moving out of the country during the war. Some 100 000 people emigrated to overseas countries in the period between the two world wars, and ten or so thousand to European countries. During World War II and directly after it - from 1941 to 1947 - another 250 000 people left Croatia. From 1948 until 1981, 325 000 people emigrated permanently, with a further 45 000 people leaving between 1981 and 1991. It is estimated that a total of 1 250 000 Croats left the country between the middle of the 20th century and 1990, a least 850 000 on a permanent basis. The reasons for these migrations were not merely economic: more recent migrations have had a mainly political background. The ties these Croats retain with their original homeland were very evident during the period of creation of the democratic Croatian state and the war in which Croatian emigrants participated, either on the battlefields or by providing financial and every other means of support.

Today, Croatian emigrants can be found on all continents and they represent a powerful link in the establishment of close business and other relationships between the Republic of Croatia and their new homelands.

A permanent and lasting peace will no doubt be a stimulus for some of them to return home. Be that as it may, the Croatian people rank among those with the highest rate of emigration, but also among those who have done much to contribute to the economic, professional and scientific life of the lands in which they have re-settled.

F O L K L O R E

Various natural and historical conditions have helped to make Croatian folklore exceptionally interesting and diversified, in its basic Pannonian, Dinaric and Adriatic types. Although life has undergone great changes, folk culture, both material and spiritual, continues to be nurtured and preserved from oblivion. Ethnoparks, such as

the Kumrovec old village which is still inhabited, or the one in Sisak, have been renovated. Old oak porches, small river boats with their typical Croatian angles, and stone cottages in the Littoral region are all preserved. Attractive tourist events are organised to bring customs out of the museum and back into life. A folklore festival is organised annually in Zagreb during the summer. Original songs,

dances and costumes from all the Croatian regions can be seen there. This is one of the rare places where one can see, at the same time and in the same place, the Istrian single-reed pipe, the sopila, Lika bagpipes, the silky Dalmatian urban costume, the Dinaric trousers made from homespun, and the richly embroidered Pannonian cloth, Slavonian sheepskin coats decorated with tiny mirrors, the short skirts with multiple petticoats from Cres, the Vrlika kolo round-dance,

those of Rijeka, Crkvenica and Samobor. Some of these customs feature the masked male dancers who wear bells hanging from their belts - the Kastav zvončari; the frightening wooden masks and the burning of the Prince of the Carnival after a jocular trial, the custom in Međimurje, the participants always managing to make people laugh with their witty comments on everyday life. Along with wedding customs and those associated with birth and death, name days and birthdays, the Slavonian *kirbaj*, or local patron saint's day

and listen to the evocative Medimurean love songs accompanied by a zither in the minor key. Croatian folk customs are linked with the seasonal changes in Nature and in life, and with the religious calendar of Roman Catholic feast days. Apart from the richest practised during Advent, Christmas, Lent and Easter, there are also very interesting customs connected with Carnival or Mardi Gras. Almost every place has its own Carnival customs, the best known being

celebration, is also of interest. Attracting visitors from all over the world, the Old Sports Olympics are held regularly in Brođanci near Valpovo; the Moreška is still danced on the island of Korčula in commemoration of the struggle against the Moors; and the Alka Games are held annually in Sinj, the horses and their riders recalling the days of chivalrous jousts and the defeat of the Turks in a battle in the early 18th century.

SOUVENIRS TO TAKE HOME

To remind them of their visit, some visitors will take home a ballpoint pen and fountain pen, first designed by a Croatian engineer called Penkala, who patented his invention in 1906. Others will choose a tie with a Croatian historical design, because the tie or cravat got its name from Croatian soldiers who wore this piece of apparel in the 17th century. Some

will select a gingerbread heart or Šestine umbrella, a *samica* which is a Slavonian musical instrument made of aromatic wood, a clay pot, an Istrian *bokaleta*, or wine goblet, lace from Lepoglava, Pag or Hvar woven from agave or century plant thread, a stone replica of the Roman arena in Pula or the Baška Inscription Stone, a photograph of Meštrović's statue of Bishop Grgur of Nin whose monumental toe is touched for good luck, a set of rosary beads from Marija Bistrica and a pledge from Međugorje, or an Adriatic shell in which the sound of the sea will be heard eternally. Some tourists take home Pag sheep-milk cheese or Lika cheese called *škripavac*, tasty kulen sausage or proscuitto, a jar of Vegeta, salted olives or lavender oil, a bottle of medicinal herb brandy called *travarica*, some good wine, a sprig of rosemary or a wreath of dried figs threaded with bay leaves. Whatever you decide to take home, you are sure to carry with you happy memories which will make you want to come back again to the lovely land of the Croats.

Continental
Cuisine

*L*egend has it that while Richard the Lionheart was returning from the Holy Land - and impatiently awaited in England - he spent a whole year at Bela Castle on the outskirts of Novi Marof, near Varaždin in Croatian Zagorje. Some explained the sumptuous feasts served there as the reason for his interrupting his journey. Varaždin, once the capital of Croatia, was called little Vienna because of its cultural life and refined culinary achievements, while fresh fish from the sea arrived every day at the seat of the Zrinski aristocratic family in Čakovec, on the other side of the River Drava. One of the members of the noble Keglević family described in his 18th century diary the fresh-water fish ponds around the castle. In order to transfer the very best of the culinary arts to local chefs, leading chefs from abroad were employed all over Croatia, as far as the estates in Baranja and Eastern Slavonia. The first chefs were Italian and French, and they were followed by Germans. Most of the ingredients they needed were readily available. The soil was generous in its diverse yield, and roads from west towards the east and from the south towards northern Europe crossed in Croatia. The knights returning from the Crusades brought back with them buckwheat, and along with spices coming on the route from the sea, there was also maize, potatoes, tomatoes, poppy-seed ... The important role of spices in trade and the high price it maintained can be seen in the historical notation about the last witch to be burned in Zagreb - because she sold a counterfeited mixture which she claimed was saffron.

*I*n his book Our First Father Adam's Sin, *Juraj Habdelic, a Jesuit from Zagreb, vented his anger of those with insatiable appetites:* There are gluttoms who waste their fortune only for prestige so that others see on their table rare titbits which are hard to come by, which they themselves perhaps would never enjoy. But, because of them, their servants and suppliers have to wear out their shoe-leather until they purchase things which no-one else has. And the greatest culinary masters have to do their utmost to prepare these goodies for guests. It really requires great skill and effort to prepare successfully various fish, Venetian confections, Italian and Spanish wine, southern fruit, poultry and all the accompaniments which go with it. The eyes feast more here now than the stomach...

*B*ut real haute cuisine can be seen, even before it found its home in France, in Belostenec's Latin-Croatian dictionary Gazophila-zyum *dating from 1740. The Baroque Kajkavian dialect terms for thyme, basil, silver beet, pheasant, a great variety of names regarding the characteristics of wine or table-ware, were lost in later standardisation of the Croatian language. They were partly revived by Bierling in 1812 in the cookery book called the* Šokač Book ... Containing 554 Recipies for All Sort of Food. *In the twentieth century, Miroslav Krleža's famous* Ballads of Petrica Kerempuh *mentions them. This serious writer could not resist writing out a recipe for Christmas turkey* a la dindek *in his cult novel* Filip Latinovicz. *Alojz Šenoa, the 19th pastry-cook from the Kaptol in Zagreb - the bishop's pastry-cook - left notes for preparing various desserts, with exotic tropical fruit, for example, and they have remained fresh from those Upper Town banquets in Zagreb up until the contemporary recipe book,* Croatian Desserts.

*C*roatian cuisine today is still very diversified and exciting because of the differences between the Croatian regions of Medimurje, Podravine, Baranja, Slavonija, Posavina, Moslavina, Prigorje, Zagorje, Banovina and Kordun, and Žumberak. Despite modern technology and techniques, more distinctively than in Mediterranean cooking, cuisine in these regions is influenced by the seasons of the year, and by more complicated preparation. The harshness of the climate leaves its mark but also the parallel traditions of simple popular cooking and the more refined aristocratic cuisine. Cooking was usually done in a separate area on a large brick and tile stove, and bread was usually baked outside in a special bread-baking oven.

*S*ummer meals usually consisted of light stewed fresh vegetables, cured meat and bacon, and milk products, while more high calorie meals with beans, potatoes, pickled cabbage, and cured meat were eaten during the winter. Polenta with butter, milk or ghoulash were eaten throughout the year. In the continental part of Croatia, almost as in Slavic times, cabbage and vegetables are pickled, and meat, usually pork, is first marinated in salted brine and then cured by smoking. Smoked ham, bacon, kulen sausage, and other cut dried sausages would be served with fresh cottage cheese or cured cheese made from cow's milk, and with sliced onion. North western Croatia prefers cooked cured pork hock served with horseradish, while poultry is a favourite throughout the entire region: turkey in Croatian Zagorje, and geese and ducks in Turopolje, Medimurje, Podravina, Posavina, and Moslavina. Chickens even found themselves in a legend about a famous victory of the people of Đurđevac against the Turks. After a prolonged seige, when the townspeople had completely run out of ball for their cannon, they fired chickens at the Turks, convincing them that the town still had plenty of food. The Turks then withdrew their forces. Since then, people from Đurđevac have since gone by the name Picoki, a local dialect variant of the term for chicken. Game, fresh-water fish, and mushrooms are also popular ingredients in this cuisine, and the hunter, shepherd and fisherman dishes, prepared in one pot, are particularly tasty. They are prepared in the open during work on the farms, just as in former nomadic times. Historians believe that mlinci also date from that period.

*T*here are fascinating customs connected with the preparation and sharing of recipes with neighbouring countries: in the east and the north with Hungary (paprika, highly spiced foods), in the west with Vienna and central European cuisine as a whole, and the influences from the east, particularly Arab and Turkish (drawn dough in the central European strudels and štrukli, a speciality in north western Croatia, and sarma, cabbage rolls filled with meat and rice).

*I*f travelling in continental Croatia, one should not miss trying Slavonian kulen sausage, Medimurean lard spread, prge from Podravina or turoš from Medimurje, štrukle served in any of the variants, chicken soup with home-made noodles, Samobor garlic sausages with Samobor mustard, blood sausages with baked pickled cabbage, Zagorje turkey with mlinci, fish paprika stew, shepherd's stew, turnip with beans, barley, duck with buckwheat stuffing, roast meat in a pak, Stubica roast meat, Varaždin feast, kotlovina barbecue, Zagreb scallop or Samobor cutlets. And then there are the sweets and cakes: walnut and poppy-seed roll, doughnuts, sače, Prigorje perica, Zagorje pumpkin-pie with poppy-seed, greblicu, tenk zlevku, bihop's bread, bear-paw biscuits, wonderful cakes, any of the strudels, and not-to-be-missed Croatian pancakes with cheese filling which are then covered with cream and baked.

Cold hors-d'oeuvres

Work was hard in the old days, and food had to be nourishing and rich in calories. It was treated with respect. Foodstuffs were carefully stored and preserved in seasons when they were plentiful, so they would keep. This applied to food of animal origin as well as to fruit and vegetables. Skill acquired through centuries was demonstrated at various gatherings such as harvesting, celebrations and holidays, when the best dishes were served in considerable quantities. In Slavonia, for example, kulen sausage was cured for more than six months and then served at very special occasions for very special guests. Ham was served at Easter all over Croatia, either smoked or boiled. Plowing and vineyard hoeing

were occasions when smoked bacon was a must.

Side dishes made from milk products and vegetables accentuated the taste of cured meat
which was often served with pickled cucumbers, peppers, paprika or aivar (a spicy relish
made from red peppers). Other frequent favourites were onions and garlic, which went
very well with various types of fresh cottage cheese, often served with sour cream, and
with additional seasoning in the Podravina region.

Nothing goes better with such delicacies than home-made bread made from wheat, maize,
rye or mixed flour, baked in an old-fashioned bread-oven.

*I*n continental Croatia boiled smoked meat is usually served at Easter time or after heavy

field work, at weddings and at wakes. Boiled ham, or ham baked in bread is usually served

with cured, smoked and boiled pork shank. Sometimes one also finds smoked tongue, garlic sausag-

es, and pressed sausage. Freshly grated horseradish adds to the special aromas and tastes of these

products, along with new spring and summer vegetables - peppers, tomatoes, hot peppers, spring

onions or shallots.

The tart refreshing taste of fresh cottage cheese, served with sour cream is a favourite, as well as air-

dried cheese moulded into small domes, called prga.

Beef Soup

(serves 6)

750 g. (1.5 lb.) beef with bone
1.5 l. (2 pints) water
1 small onion
40 g. (1.5 oz.) carrots
20 g. (2/3 oz.) celeriac (root and leaves)
40 g. (1.5 oz.) parsley root with leaves
Vegeta
salt
4 - 5 peppercorns

Put the washed meat into lukewarm water. When the water comes to the boil, add the peppercorns, carrots, parsley root and celeriac. Cut the onion in half and scorch on the hob without peeling. Add to the soup. Cook the covered soup over a low heat for about two hours. After the meat is half cooked, add the salt. When the meat is tender, add a small quantity of cold water and set aside for a few minutes. Remove the meat from the soup. Strain the soup through a fine sieve.

Before serving, bring the soup to the boil. Cook home-made noodles or dumplings in the soup. When they are ready, add the chopped parsley.

(1 serving amounts to 108/454 cal/J)

Tip:

For a really tasty soup, take care that it simmers over a low heat i.e. simmer gently.

For the meat to leave its "strength and value" in the soup, place it in cold water when cooking begins; for the meat to be juicy and tender, place it in hot water.

Horseradish Sauce

Prepare the sauce by first putting two slices of stale white bread in a small amount of hot soup. Press through a sieve and add 60 g. (2.5 oz.) of grated horseradish, a few drops of vinegar and oil, and a pinch of salt.

Chicken Broth

(serves 6)

1 hen, 40 g. (1.5 oz.) carrots
40 g. (1.5 oz.) parsley root and leaves
20 g. (2/3 oz.) celeriac (root), 20 g. (2/3 oz.)
onion, 1.5 litres (2 pints) cold water
salt, peppercorns

Place the cleaned and washed hen in cold water together with the carrots, parsley root, celeriac, a few peppercorns and slices of onion scorched on the stove plate. Add the salt and let the soup simmer until the meat becomes tender. Take the hen out of the soup and strain the soup through a sieve. If there is too much fat on the soup surface, leave it to cool and then remove the fat.

If liked, cook some home-made noodles in the soup. Garnish with chopped parsley before serving.

(1 serving amounts to 98/412 Cal/C)

Tip:

An older hen gives a more tasty soup. If the meat does not become tender after 2 - 3 hours of cooking, add a small amount of brandy.

Dill Sauce

Lightly fry 2 tablespoons of flour in 40 g. (1.5 oz.) heated butter. Pour in 500 ml. (20 fl. oz.) of soup. Add a small amount of Vegeta. Cook for about 5 minutes, stirring constantly, until the sauce thickens. Add lemon juice, 100 ml. (4 fl. oz.) sour cream. When almost done, add a bunch of finely chopped dill.

*B*roths were made for special occasions, as an introduction to a festive dinner or supper, particularly at weddings. cuts were not used in soup making. Small pieces of fowl or bones, and beef and veal pieces containing fat were usually used. When very large quantities were cooked, all types of meat were used, but then the cooked meat was served as the first course, immediately after the soup. Rice dishes, boiled potatoes, or vegetables cooked in the soup were served with the meat, as well as various sauces. This was usually tomato sauce, horseradish sauce, dill sauce or cucumber sauce...

Creamed Bean Soup

(serves 4-6)

250 g. (9 oz.) cooked beans
2 g. (2/3 oz.) smoked bacon
2 g. (2/3 oz.) oil
1 tablespoon tomato puree
1 celeriac stalk with leaves, bay leaf
1 litre (1.75 pints) water
salt, pepper
1 tablespoon Vegeta
1tablespoon plain flour
2 garlic cloves, parsley, vinegar

Cut the bacon into small pieces and lightly fry in oil. Add the tomato puree, celeriac leaves, bay leaf and cooked beans. Add water sufficient to cover the beans, boil briefly and then puree the ingredients. Add about a litre of water, salt, pepper to taste, Vegeta and bring to the boil. Just before the soup is cooked, add the tablespoon of flour mixed in a small quantity of water, the chopped parsley and garlic, and vinegar to taste.
Serve in bowls with fried bread croutons..
(1 serving amounts to 280/1176 Cal/J)

Chicken Ragout Soup

(serves 4-6)

200 g. (7 oz.) chicken (white meat)
50 g. (2 oz.) peas, 100 g. (4 oz.) cauliflower
50 g. (2 oz.) champignons (button mushrooms)
nutmeg, salt, pepper
100 g. (4 oz.) root vegetables (carrots, celeriac, parsley), 40 g. (1.5 oz.) butter
20 g. (2/3 oz.) flour, 1 egg yolk
2 tablespoons sour cream, lemon juice
1 cube chicken soup, parsley leaves

Dice the chicken and root vegetables. Lightly sauté the chicken in butter, and then the prepared root vegetables. Add the cauliflower and peas. Salt lightly, sprinkle with flour and add water. Add the chicken soup cube and leave to simmer slowly.
Sauté the sliced champignons in butter, salt to taste, and add to the soup. Pepper to taste, add some grated nutmeg. When almost cooked, add the egg yolk mixed with sour cream and some chopped parsley leaves. Add some lemon juice to taste.

(1 serving amounts to 212/890 Cal/J)

Creamed Vegetable Soup

(serves 4-6)

2 carrots, 2 parsley roots
40 g. (1.5 oz.) celeriac root
100 g. (4 oz.) spinach, 30 g. (1 oz.) butter
20 g. (2/3 oz.) flour, nutmeg, salt, pepper
100 ml. (4 fl. oz.) sour cream, 1 egg yolk
1 vegetable soup cube

Cook the diced root vegetables in a small amount of water. When almost soft, add the spinach. When cooked, leave to cool and put through a sieve. Heat the butter, sprinkle with flour, stir above the heat and then add water (use the water in which the vegetables were cooked). Add fresh water so the quantity of liquid amounts to 1.4 l (2.3 pints). Add the pureed vegetables, soup cube, some grated nutmeg and pepper, and let it all come to the boil. Add salt to taste and the sour cream into which the egg yolk has been stirred.
Serve the soup in bowls, adding fried bread croutons per taste.

(1 serving amounts to 142/596 Cal/J).

Soup Prežgana

(serves 4-6)

30 g (1 oz.) flour
40 g. (1.5 oz.) oil or butter
bay leaf
caraway seeds
salt

Fry the flour in oil or butter until it turns golden brown. Add a litre (1.75 pints) of cold water, and take care that there are no lumps. Add the bay leaf and caraway seeds, salt to taste and cook for about 20 minutes. Prežgana soup can be served with an egg whisked until fluffy and then added to the soup and boiled briefly, or with fried bread croutons.

(1 serving amounts to 98/412 Cal/J)

Although broth was the type of soup most often served at festive occasions, cream soups were also very popular. Chicken ragout soup, is the typical middle-class soup, which has its twins in soups prepared according to the same recipe, but with veal or lamb meat substituted for the chicken. For practical purposes vegetable cream soup was made from vegetables in season available at markets in certain periods of the year. This type of soup was always new and different, but always very tasty. Creamed bean soup is especially interesting, as well as the always popular tomato soup, similar to prežgana soup, because it may be served with fried bread croutons or cooked beaten eggs. These soups were served in both country and town homes... There were times when the favourite version was soup cooked with corn flour. As these filling soups may be supplemented with various additions, they are a very nourishing meal. They were usually prepared when heavy field work was in progress and when there was not enough time for cooking. Other simple dishes were served such as plum or apricot dumplings, pastries with jam filling, dumplings with poppy-seeds... Or cottage cheese, sour cream, onions, sliced smoked bacon, ham, and sausages. Today these soups are made stronger and tastier by adding Vegeta, the universal food additive, or by using soup cubes.

Boiled Štrukli (shtrukli)

(serves 6-8)

Pastry:
500 g./ 1 lb. 1 2/3 oz. flour, 1 egg
2 tablespoons oil, salt, 1 tablespoon mild
vinegar, lukewarm water

Filling:
100 - 150 g. / 3 1/2 - 5 oz. butter, 4 eggs
600 g. / 1 1/4 lb. fresh cottage cheese
100 ml / 3 1/2 oz sour cream, salt

Topping:
80 g. / 2 3/4 oz. butter, 50 g./ 1 2/3 oz. bread crumbs

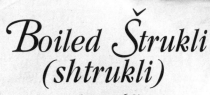

Sift the flour. Prepare some lukewarm water. Make a small depression in the centre of the sifted flour. Put the salt, oil and one egg into it. Mix with a knife, slowly adding the lukewarm water combined with vinegar. Knead the dough until completely smooth. Divide the dough into three equal parts, brush them with oil, cover with a heated bowl and set aside for about half an hour.

In the meantime prepare the filling:

Mix the softened butter with the strained and creamed cheese, whisked eggs and a little salt until light and fluffy. Add the sour cream.

Cover a table with a cloth. Flour the cloth well. Roll out one of the dough pieces with a rolling pin, and continue stretching the dough with floured hands towards the edges of the table until it becomes thin. Cut off any thick edges. Leave the stretched dough to dry for a while. Then sprinkle it with part of the melted butter. Spread one-third of the prepared filling over one-half of the prepared dough and roll into a strudel. Press the roll every 10 cm/4 inches with a large wooden spoon handle, and then cut out the štrukli with the edge of a plate. The edges of the dough must be tightly sealed. Cook the štrukli in salted boiling water for 15 - 20 minutes, but do not cook large quantities at the same time. Take the štrukli out of the water with a slotted spoon and arrange them on a plate. Fry the bread crumbs in oil briefly and pour over the štrukli. Štrukli prepared in this manner can be served as a separate dish. On festive occasions they can be served with wild game or some other meat dish with sauce.
(1 serving amounts to 573/2407 cal/J)

Tip:
You can serve cooked štrukli with bread crumbs as a dessert, but in this case less salt is added into the filling, and the štrukli are sprinkled with sugar.

As the German name štrukli indicates, this is a dish which is considered in some parts to be the same as strudel, or similar to it. But, what is basic for all štrukli is that they are prepared from drawn dough, filled and rolled. They may be savoury or sweet; boiled, baked, and then boiled and baked; they are served in soups, or as hors-d'oeuvres and desserts They can be the main dish or the independent snack. Because of their being universal, very tasty, and suitable for freezing, they are a favourite dish in modern Croatian cuisine.

Baked Štrukli

Štrukli prepared in the manner described on page 46 can then be baked in the oven or gratinated. If you wish to bake the štrukli, arrange them in a buttered baking dish or oven-proof casserole. Pour some sour cream over them and place in the oven. Bake at 180 - 200°C /Gas Mark 4 / 350° - 400°F /Gas Mark 6 for about 40 minutes. The štrukli will be tastier if covered with small pieces of butter before baking.

(1 serving amounts to 272/1142 cal/C)

Green Štrukli

(serves 6-8)

Prepare the štrukli dough according to recipe on page 46. Make a Swiss chard or spinach filling for the štrukli in the following manner:

300 g. (11 oz.) Swiss chard or spinach
40 g. (1.5 oz.) oil
40 g. (1.5 oz.) onion
salt, pepper
100 g. (4 oz.) butter, 2 eggs
500 g. (18 oz.) fresh cottage cheese
100 g. (4 oz.) sour cream
2 cloves garlic, Vegeta

Cook (blanch) the Swiss chard or spinach briefly in boiling water, strain and chop finely. Fry the chopped onion in oil until yellow, add the prepared Swiss chard or spinach, Vegeta, salt and pepper and cook briefly, then leave to cool. Mix the butter until fluffy, add the egg yolks, sour cream, the strained and creamed cottage cheese and chopped garlic. Mix with the prepared Swiss chard or spinach. Last of all fold in the egg whites beaten into peaks. If the filling is too thin, stir in some semolina or bread crumbs. Roll out the štrukli dough, draw it out, sprinkle with melted butter and spread the filling. Roll up and cut out the štrukli with a plate edge. Boil in salted water for about 15 minutes. Take the cooked štrukli out of the water with a slotted spoon and arrange them on a warm plate. You can serve this type of štrukli as warm hors d'oeuvres with only a sour cream or butter topping, and they can also be served together with meat and sauce dishes.

(1 serving 298/1252 Cal/J)

Štrukli Soup

(serves 4-8)

4 - 8 štrukli prepared per recipe on page 46
4 tablespoons oil, 50 g. (2 oz.) onion
1 teaspoon sweet red paprika
2 tablespoons sour cream
parsley, salt, Vegeta
1 litre (1.75 pints) water

Heat the oil in a deep and wide saucepan and sauté the finely chopped onion. Immediately add the sweet red paprika and the water. Add the salt and Vegeta. As soon as the soup comes to the boil, place the prepared štrukli side by side in the soup, and allow to simmer about 15 minutes. Add the sour cream and chopped parsley. Take the štrukli out of the soup with a slotted spoon, place them in soup plates, pour the soup over them and serve.

(1 serving amounts to 282/1184 cal/J)

Oven-baked Štrukli

Prepare štrukli according to the basic recipe on page 46. Boil them in salted water until they are half-cooked. Take them out of the water with a slotted spoon, drain them and arrange in an oven-proof casserole or baking dish and pour sweet cream over them. Place in a preheated oven and bake about 20 minutes at 180° - 200°C/350° - 400°F/Gas Mark 4.
These štrukli may be served either savoury or sweet.

Š trukli are a very popular speciality in almost all of the Northwest Croatia. Although today the best known today are štrukli with fresh cheese, Samobor is the town where štrukli are prepared with green vegetables. In Hrvatsko Zagorje (Croatian Zagorje) they were filled with a pumpkin and poppyseed filling, and in the Podravina region with a buckwheat filling. In the Medimurje region they were prepared with some twenty different types of fillings, even including a millet filling.

*P*asta is a favourite in all Croatian regions. Today, when one can buy ready-made pasta, dry or frozen pasta, the home-made article is highly prized. This is partly due to the many possibilities of preparing it : with egg or without, using different types of flour, and in a wide variety of shapes. Whether only boiled or additionally baked afterwards, it is very nutritious, easily digestible, and can be combined with various other foodstuffs in different dishes. Although Italian pasta is preferred today, various home-made noodles, mlinci and other differently shaped pasta are still the favourite dish of many Croatians.

"Ozalj" Noodles with Mushrooms

(serves 4-6)

300 g. (11 oz.) broad noodles
3 tablespoons oil
1 small onion
400 g. (14 oz.) fresh mushrooms (various types)
oregano
Vegeta
100 ml. (4 fl. oz.) white wine
2 cloves garlic
salt, pepper

30 g. (1 oz.) butter
150 g. (5 oz.) fresh cottage cheese
200 ml. (8 fl. oz.) cream
1 egg yolk, parsley leaves

Cook the noodles in salted water and drain them. Fry the chopped onion and sliced mushrooms in heated oil. Add oregano, Vegeta, pour in the wine and sauté until the mushrooms are cooked. When almost cooked, add chopped garlic and pepper to taste.

Melt the butter in a wide saucepan. Add the cooked noodles, cottage cheese, sour cream, egg yolk and the prepared mushrooms. Mix gently and heat well. Serve sprinkled with chopped parsley.

(1 serving amounts to 589/2474 Cal/J)

Noodles with Fresh Cottage Cheese

(serves 4-6)

350 g. (12 oz.) broad noodles
2 tablespoons oil
80 g. (3 oz.) smoked bacon
250 g. (9 oz.) fresh cottage cheese
200 ml. (8 fl. oz.) sour cream
powdered red pepper, salt

Cook the noodles in salted water.
Fry the diced bacon in oil. Add the drained noodles, sprinkle with powdered red paprika. Blend all the ingredients well, warm the noodles, fold in gently the creamed cottage cheese, place in a buttered heat-resistant casserole. Top with slightly salted sour cream. Bake for about 20 minutes at 200°C/400°F/ Gas Mark 6.
Fresh lettuce salad compliments this dish.
(1 serving amounts to 508/2134 Cal/J)

Noodles with Ham and Champignons (Button mushrooms)

(serves 4-6)

350 g. (12 oz.) wide noodles
80 g. butter or margarine
200 g. (7 oz.) cooked ham
200 g. (7 oz.) champignons
1 tablespoon flour
450 ml. (18 fl. oz.) milk
salt
pepper
parsley
40 g. (1.5 oz) grated cheese
200 ml. (8 fl. oz.) cream
Vegeta

Cook the noodles in boiling salted water. In the meantime, fry the ham cut into strips and the champignons cut into slices. Braise for about 10 minutes, sprinkle with flour and a pinch of Vegeta. Pour milk over these ingredients and cook some more. When almost cooked, add pepper, chopped parsley, and a small amount of grated cheese. Strain the cooked noodles and place in the sauce. Pour cream over this and blend well.
(1 serving amounts to 715/3003 Cal/J)

*A*though it is considered that the Croatian word for pancakes - palačinke - comes from the Hungarian word "palacsinta", there is no doubt that the roots of the word originate from the Latin - placenta. So it is probable that palačinke - rounds of batter baked on hot plates - appeared in the Croatian cuisine at the same time as else-where. Today pancakes are an international dish, in many cases a fast food. In Croatia, they have preserved their national characteristics, whether savoury or sweet. They are equally loved whether prepared with cream, mineral water, melted butter, a dot of home-made bran-dy or rum. They are especially tasty with cottage cheese, baked in the oven. Although very simple, this dish allows many possibilities and a rich palette of tastes and aromas.

Basic Pancakes

200 g. (7 oz.) flour
2 eggs
400 ml. (16 fl. oz.) milk
salt, oil for frying

Mix the eggs in a deep bowl, salt to taste, and add the milk and flour alternately, mix-ing constantly until the batter becomes smooth and liquid. Heat the pancake pan well, add a little oil, heat again. Pour a small amount of batter into the centre of the pan using a ladle so that it spreads uniformly over the complete surface. Fry the pancakes on both sides.

You can make different fillings for the pan-cakes, to taste.

Fried Breaded Pancakes with Turkey Filling

(serves 4)

8 pancakes
Filling:
250 g. (9 oz.) turkey or chicken
1 teaspoon Vegeta, 40 g. (1.5 oz.) butter
nutmeg, 1 pickled cucumber
1 pickled red pepper
salt, pepper, 100 ml. (4 fl. oz.) sour cream
flour, eggs, bread crumbs, frying oil

Dice the turkey or chicken, sprinkle with Vegeta, salt to taste, mix, and braise this mix-ture in hot butter. When the meat is almost cooked, add nutmeg, finely chopped cucum-ber and pepper, and the sour cream. Place a spoonful of the filling on each pancake, fold twice towards the centre, then roll up. Roll the filled pancakes in flour, dip them in a raw egg mixture, finally roll in bread crumbs. Fry in oil on all sides until golden yellow.

Arrange the pancakes on a hot plate. Serve with sauce tartar or fresh salad.

(1 serving amounts to 512/2150 Cal/J)

Pancakes with Mushroom Filling
(serves 4)

8 pancakes
Filling:
4 tablespoons oil, 20 g. (2/3 oz.) butter
60 g. (2 oz.) onion, 200 g. (7 oz.) mushrooms (champignons), 1 teaspoon Vegeta
1 g. (1/2 oz.) flour, salt, pepper
nutmeg, 1 garlic clove, parsley
150 ml. (5 fl. oz.) sour cream

Fry the finely chopped onion in butter, add the sliced mushrooms, and braise together. Sprinkle with flour, stir in Vegeta, pepper, grated nutmeg, a pinch of salt and finely chopped garlic. Add some water, bring to the boil and cook some more. Finally, when cooked, add chopped parsley and 50 ml. (2 fl. oz.) sour cream.

Fill the pancakes with this filling and fold them. Arrange the pancakes on plates covered with a thin film of sour cream.

(1 serving amounts to 430/1806 Cal/J)

Baked Pancakes with Meat Filling
(serves 4)

8 pancakes
Filling:
250 g. (9 oz.) minced meat
100 g. (4 oz.) onion
5 tablespoons oil
1 tablespoon Vegeta
200 g. (7 oz.) fresh tomato
salt
pepper
marjoram
Topping:
200 ml. (8 fl. oz.) sour cream
2 eggs
salt
nutmeg
40 g. (1.5 oz.) grated cheese

Put the chopped onion and minced meat in heated oil, braise briefly, adding small amounts of water as necessary. Then add the peeled and sliced tomatoes, Vegeta, salt, pepper and marjoram. Braise until the water evaporates. Fill pancakes with this filling, roll them up and arrange side by side in an oven-proof casserole or buttered baking tin. Prepare the topping : mix the egg yolks and sour cream, grated cheese, grated nutmeg, and egg whites whisked into peaks. Bake for about 15 minutes in a hot oven. Serve as hot hors-d'oeuvres or as a main course with fresh salad.

(1 serving amounts to 553/2323 Cal/J)

Note:

You can use this recipe and substitute simple and budget-saving fillings by using leftover meat, ham or the like.

Spring Vegetable Stew

(serves 4-6)

800 g. (1.75 lb.) various vegetables (carrots, kohlrabi, green peas)
200 g. (7 oz.) potatoes
several fresh cabbage leaves
parsley leaves
50 g. (2 oz.) onion
40 g. (2 oz.) oil
10 g. (1/2 oz.) sugar
20 g. (2/3 oz.) flour
salt
pepper
lemon juice

Cut the carrots, kohlrabi and potatoes into narrow strips, and the cabbage into wide strips. Shell the peas. Fry the sugar in oil briefly, add chopped onion, and cook until glassy. Add the prepared vegetables and cook until soft. Add water or soup made of a soup cube when needed, and stir occasionally. Sprinkle the stew with flour, salt, pepper. Add some more liquid, if necessary, and boil briefly. Finally, sprinkle with chopped parsley, and add lemon juice to taste.

(1 serving amounts to 166/697 Cal/J)

Pumpkin Stew

(serves 4-6)

700 g. (1.6 lb.) pumpkin
2 tablespoons mild apple or other vinegar
40 g. (1.5 oz.) oil, 1 small onion
1-2 cloves garlic, 200 g. (7 oz.) fresh tomatoes
or 10 g. (1/2 oz.) tomato concentrate, caraway
seeds, salt, Vegeta, 50 ml. (2 fl. oz.) sour cream
10 g. (1/2 oz.) flour, parsley

Roughly grate the peeled pumpkin and sprinkle with vinegar. Sauté the chopped onion in oil until it turns golden yellow and then add the chopped garlic, grated pumpkin, and the peeled and chopped fresh tomato or tomato concentrate. Add caraway seeds, a little Vegeta and salt. Cover and stew. When some liquid evaporates and the pumpkin turns soft, stir in the sour cream mixed with flour. Cook briefly and finally sprinkle with chopped parsley. This pumpkin stew may be served with minced meat, cooked beef or with mashed potatoes covered with fried bread crumbs.

(1 serving amounts to 124/521 Cal/J)

Savoy Cabbage Stew

(serves 4-6)

1 kg (2 lb.) Savoy cabbage
300 g. (11 oz.) potatoes, 1 teaspoon Vegeta
salt, pepper, 20 g. (2/3 oz.) oil
40 g. (1.5 oz.) smoked bacon
40 g. (1.5 oz.) onion, 20 g. (2/3 oz.) flour
2 cloves garlic, caraway seeds

Cut the Savoy cabbage into four, remove damaged and hard parts, cut into wide strips. Peel the potatoes and dice. Put these ingredients together in a pan and pour some hot water over them. Sprinkle with Vegeta, add a pinch of salt, cover the pan and simmer.
Fry some sliced bacon and chopped onion in hot oil. Add this to the cooked Savoy cabbage. When almost cooked, add the flour dissolved in a little water, chopped garlic and pepper to taste. Chopped caraway seeds may be added to taste.
Serve with minced meat balls.
(1 serving amounts to 158/664 Cal/J)

S tew is the word that may describe the manner of cooking or the very dish. This dish may be served as an independent meal or with meat as was the case in the past in more prosperous households. In other cases bones or bacon skin were added to the vegetables and cooked instead of meat. When browned flour is added, this meal is very filling. Before refrigerators were invented, stews depended on the vegetables in season. Therefore, the lighter stews cooked in spring and summer contained fresh vegetables, whereas the more filling ones prepared in winter were often based on preserves.

Stewed Sauerkraut (pickled cabbage)

(serves 4-6)

750 g. (1.75 lb.) sauerkraut
4 tablespoons oil
30 g. (1 oz.) cured bacon
1 small onion, 2 garlic cloves
juniper berry, 1 teaspoon caraway seeds
1 bay leaf, 1 tablespoon Vegeta

Fry the diced bacon and chopped onion in oil. Add the sauerkraut, (if too sour, wash and drain it), juniper berries, caraway seeds, bay leaf and Vegeta. Simmer until the sauerkraut is cooked. Add water when necessary. When it is almost done, stir in the chopped garlic.

Serve the stewed sauerkraut with blood sausages, baking sausages or garlic sausages.
(1 serving amounts to 185/777 Cal/J)

*H*ot-pot dishes are favourites which can be eaten with only a spoon. In the past this was the usual everyday food in country homes in wintertime. Cured meat or bacon, sausages, or corn mush could always be added. In Germany they have Eintopf, the English have Stew, the French Pot au feu, the Slovenes enolončnice .. dishes prepared in one pot. Probably over a fire in the old days.

Turnip and Bean Stew

(serves 4-6)

1 kg (2 lb.) pickled turnip
500 g. (18 oz.) beans, 80 g. (3 oz.) fat
40 g. (1.5 oz.) flour, 80 g. (3 oz.) onion
garlic, salt, peppercorns, bay leaf
1 tablespoon Vegeta

Briefly cook the beans previously soaked in water, drain them and cook again in fresh water. Cook the turnip separately with the bay leaf, several peppercorns and the Vegeta. Add the cooked turnip to the cooked beans. Fry the chopped onion in fat, add the flour, pour in some cold water, and add to the beans and turnip. Add the chopped garlic, salt to taste, and cook briefly.

The turnip and bean stew will be tastier if you add some raw or smoked pig knuckles, or some other kind of cured meat.

(1 serving amounts to 490/2058 Cal/J).

Thick Barley and Bean Soup

(serves 4)

150 g. (5 oz.) barley
200 g. (7 oz.) beans
400 g. (14 oz.) smoked spare rib
2 carrots
1 parsley (root and sprigs)
30 g. (1 oz.) celeriac (root)
4 cloves garlic
3 tablespoons oil
salt, peppercorns
bay leaf
marjoram
vinegar

Briefly cook the previously soaked beans, drain, add new water and simmer until the beans are cooked. Season with salt just before the beans are cooked.

Cook the cleaned and washed barley at the same time. Cook the washed spare rib separately. When cooked, bone the meat and cut it into cubes.

Dice the carrots, parsley and celeriac root, and sauté in oil. When necessary, add more water (use the water the spare ribs have been cooked in). Add the bay leaf and the marjoram.

Place the cooked beans, barley, cubed cooked meat and the sautéed vegetables into a large casserole. Add some water (use the water the spare rib had been cooked in). Add salt and pepper to taste, chopped garlic and parsley, continue cooking.

Add some vinegar to taste.

(amounts to 482/2024 cal/J)

I *t is a rare festive occasion and festive table - particu-*

larly at Christmas-time - that does not feature poultry dishes (turkey,

duck, geese, chicken), or mlinci. Historians consider mlinci, which are most often made without

eggs or fat, to be the predecessor of leavened dough. In the past when they were baked on country home hot

stove plates, they were part of a small family ritual, especially for children. Today they are retained as a taste

of the past.

Preparing Mlinci

Prepare a dough from flour and lukewarm salted water. The dough should not be too firm in consistency. Knead well.

Divide this dough into 4 - 5 lumps. Roll each one out into a round shape, not too thin. Bake each piece separately over a hot grid in the oven.

Break up each baked piece into smaller pieces. Place the pieces in slightly salted boiling water and drain immediately.

Tip:

You may prepare mlinci several days in advance. Store mlinci in a cloth bag, close the bag and store in a dry place. Prepare them just before sitting down to the meal.

Duck with Mlinci

(serves 6)

1 duck (about 2 kg / 4.5 lb.)
salt, 1 tablespoon Vegeta
lard
Mlinci:
350 g. (12 oz.) flour
salt, water

Wash the duck, and rub it with a salt and Vegeta mixture inside and out. Let it rest like this several hours, or overnight. Before roasting, spread lard over the duck, place it in a baking tin to which you have added a little water. Place the baking tin into a heated oven and bake slowly. Roast the duck slowly, basting it in its own juices. The oven temperature should be between 180°C (350°F) /Gas Mark 4 and 200°C (400°F)/ Gas Mark 6. When the duck is done, take it out and place it on a board.

Cut into pieces.

Leave the roasting juices in the tin. Remove the surplus fat. Place mlinci into the tin, mix and bake briefly.

Arrange the duck pieces and mlinci on a large plate, garnish and serve.

(1 serving amounts to 878/3688 Cal/J)

The turkey in the following reci-
pe was not named "purgerica"
only by chance. The men and women of
Zagreb are often referred to as purger
and purgerica respectively (a variation
of the German term, Burger), and the
recipe is a variant of an old Christmas
dish from the Zagreb suburbs. There were
peasant women in those times who
served in rich city homes, taking back
home with them culinary experience.

This turkey dish is especially interesting
for its rich and unusual stuffing, the usu-
al one being made from chestnuts, ap-
ples, bacon, lemon, various spices...

Turkey
"Purgerica"

(serves 12)

1 turkey (about 5 kg. / 10 lb.)
1 kg. (2 lb.) tripe
750 g. pork scrag end
350 g. (12 oz.) beef and pork
1 piece of raw pork skin (or 1 sheet ge-latine)
soup vegetables
bay leaf
2 stale bread rolls
1 onion, 2 eggs
parsley, salt
ground pepper and peppercorns
Levisticum officinale (herb)
nutmeg
pork lard
1 tablespoon Vegeta

Rub salt into the turkey and leave it to rest overnight. Wash the tripe well and boil it in water with the bay leaf and peppercorns. In another saucepan boil the beef, pork and fat pork meet, pork skin and soup vegetables. Pour some soup over the stale bread rolls.

Put the cooked and chilled meat, tripe, vegetables and moistened rolls through a mincing machine. Add chopped onion and parsley, egg yolks, pepper, salt, Levisticum officinale (ljupčac-herb), nutmeg and Vegeta and blend well all the ingredients. Add egg whites whisked to the peaks stage, and fold in gently. Fill the turkey opening with this stuffing, and close the opening with toothpicks or sew with thread. Brush with pork fat and roast in the oven.

Baste occasionally with water and roasting juices. Roast about 3 hours, until the meat is tender. Carve the turkey. Take the stuffing

out of the opening and cut into slices. Arrange on a hot plate and pour the roasting
juices over the meat and stuffing. Serve
mlinci as a side dish.

(1 serving amounts to 1120/4704 Cal/J)

61

Goose Turopolje Style

(serves 6-8)

1 goose (about 2.5 kg./5 lb.)
500 g. (18 oz.) corn grits
goose liver and gizzard
4 tablespoons oil
1 onion
1 tablespoon Vegeta
1 - 2 cloves
3 - 4 cloves garlic
salt, pepper
ground sweet red paprika

*I*n the past, poultry was always served at festive occasions. Geese and ducks were usually raised along the banks of rivers such as the Drava, Mura, Sava, Kupa, Lonja ... Stories about white flocks, soft eiderdown coverlets, pillows, the feather trade, cured geese, and most of all - goose liver are all rather nostalgic. Geese and ducks were force-fed weeks before holidays such as Christmas or St. Martin's Day.

Clean, wash and dry the goose. Sprinkle it with a mixture of salt and Vegeta inside and out a couple of hours prior to roasting (preferably the day before). Before roasting the goose, pour oil over it. Add water to the roasting tin, and put in a preheated oven to roast at 200°C/400°F/Gas Mark 6. Baste from time to time with its own juices, and add water to the baking tin to keep the roast juicy.

While the goose is roasting, prepare the side dish. Add salt and Vegeta, chopped liver and gizzard, lightly fried onion and garlic to 750 ml./32 fl. oz. water. Also add the cloves, pepper and ground sweet red paprika, and boil until the liver and gizzard become soft. Just before cooking is completed, pour in the corn grits and cook, stirring constantly. If the mixture becomes too thick and hard in consistency, add a little hot water. After removing the goose from the tin, pour the cooked mixture directly into the roasting juices, place the goose on top and roast for about 30 more minutes.

Carve the roast goose for serving, arrange on a plate together with the corn grits mash. Serve with any salad of the season.

(1 serving amounts to 685/2877 Cal/J)

Tip:

If there is too much fat after roasting the goose, remove some before adding the corn grits mixture.

Duck Međimurje Style
(serves 4-6)

1 duck (about 2 kg./4.5 lb.)	
200 g. (7 oz.) buckwheat porridge	
100 g. (4 oz.) pork fat or lard	
1 onion	
1 duck or chicken liver	
parsley	
salt	
pepper	
Vegeta	

Clean, wash and dry the duck. Sprinkle with salt on the outside and rub with Vegeta around the inside.

Clean the buckwheat and wash it in plenty of lukewarm water. Boil it briefly in salted water and drain. Fry the chopped onion and liver in part of the fat, add the drained buckwheat porridge, and pepper to taste. Blend well, remove from the heat source and sprinkle with chopped parsley. Then stuff the duck with this mixture and place in a roasting tin with the remaining fat. Roast at about 200°C/400°F/Gas Mark 6.

Baste the duck with its own juices. Add a little water occasionally to keep the roast juicy.

Carve the duck, arrange the pieces on a heated plate, add the buckwheat porridge and pour the roasting juices over the dish. Serve with sauerkraut salad, beetroot salad or some other salad of choice.

(1 serving amounts to 862/3620 Cal/J)

Roast Sucking Pig

An old Croatian saying is that "there is no bird like a suckling pig". Especially esteemed is the meat that "still has the aroma of milk". Suckling pigs are roasted whole, the smaller ones in old baker's ovens, and the larger ones over a spit. Preparation time is often an introduction to many hours of company round the table. This roast is usually prepared for large, official and personal celebrations, and it is a must on New Year's Eve. It is the custom to serve it on January first. There is a belief that the on-coming year will be successful and push forward just as a pig digs its way forward. This roast meat is served both hot and cold, but in any case the skin, or crackling should be crunchy. Potato and bean salad is usually served with the roast suckling, as well as spring onions and radishes, pickled onions and cucumbers, and the favourite side dish - French salad.

Dry the sucking pig well and sprinkle with salt. Place the sucking pig on top of cooking fat in the baking pan. Roast at about 200°C/400°F/Gas Mark 6 until the meat becomes tender, and the skin becomes golden-brown and crunchy. Baste the meat with cold oil while roasting, adding a little lukewarm water into the tin occasionally to keep it juicy.

Roast the meat for about 2 - 3 hours, depending on the meat thickness.

Carve the roast sucking pig and serve hot

with different salads.

Instead of a sucking pig, you could roast a piece of young pork. Sprinkle the meat with salt, place into the roasting tin with a little water, and place in a preheated oven. After about twenty minutes remove the meat from the oven, wipe the skin with paper tissue, and use a knife to make a criss-cross design, cutting to a depth of 3mm. Return to the oven and continue roasting. Baste the meat with cold oil during roasting so that the skin becomes crunchy and golden-brown.

French Salad
(serves 6-8)

Boil about 1 kg. (2 lb.) potatoes, a small celeriac root and several carrots. Dice finely. Mix with boiled green peas and two finely chopped or grated pickled cucumbers. Add chopped parsley, mustard, lemon juice, mayonnaise, sour cream, salt and pepper to taste, blend well.

(1 serving amounts to 206/1092 Cal/J)

Tip:
If you wish to mould the French salad attractively, add some melted gelatine.

Roast Sucking Pig Cocktail

Roast sucking pig can be served cold. Remove the meat from the bones, cut into small cubes. Arrange them on a plate and garnish with various pickled and fresh vegetables (pickled cucumbers, onions, tomatoes, paprika).

(1 serving amounts to 643/2701 Cal/J)

Stuffed Veal Breast

(Serves 4-6)

1.5 kg. (3.5 lb.) veal breast (from top end of ribs), 80 ml. (3 fl. oz.) oil
Vegeta, salt
Stuffing:
2 bread rolls
100 ml. (4 fl. oz.) milk, 2 eggs
20 g. (2/3 oz.) onion
40 g. (1.5 oz.) smoked bacon
3 tablespoons oil
salt, pepper, parsley

*R*oasts are the obligatory main part of festive dinners or suppers and weddings feasts. Christmas holidays would not be the same without roast turkey, nor St. Martin's day without roast goose. Roasts are still a symbol of meals at special gatherings. Poultry and pork were usually served in the country, and beef and veal were added in towns. More than one type of roast meat is served today, with various side dishes and salads.*

Carefully bone the meat and cut an opening for the stuffing. Wash the meat, salt and rub some Vegeta inside and out. Place the prepared stuffing in the opening and close it with toothpicks or sew with thread. Place in the oven. Baste the meat with its own juices during roasting, and add a little lukewarm water so that the meat stays juicy. Roast for about 2 hours at 200°C/400°F/Gas Mark 6 - 220°C/425°F/Gas Mark 7.

Leave the cooked meat to rest a couple of minutes. Carve it into slices carefully, and serve with boiled vegetables.

(1 serving amounts to 808/3394 Cal/J)

Stuffing:

Dice the rolls and soak in a mixture of milk and eggs. Chop the onion and bacon finely, fry in a little oil and add to the soaked rolls. Salt and pepper to taste, sprinkle with parsley and mix until all ingredients are well blended.

Note:

You can shape the veal breast and stuff it in another way. Flatten the meat out and cover with the stuffing. Make a roll and tie with thread. Continue according to previous recipe.

This veal breast roll is easier to cut and divide into portions.

Roast Pork in a Sac

(serves 4-6)

1 kg. (2 lb.) pork loin
1 pork stomach sac
1 tablespoon mustard
1 tablespoon Vegeta
4 cloves garlic
1 lemon, salt, pepper
bay leaf, oil

Wash and bone the meat. Mix together the mustard, Vegeta, crushed garlic cloves, pepper and a little salt. Spread this mixture over the meat. Arrange lemon slices over the meat, wrap well in the stomach sac and leave to rest 24 hours. Pour oil over the meat and place it in the oven to roast for about 45 minutes at 200°C/400°F/Gas Mark

6. Place the bay leaf on the meat and baste it frequently with the roasting juices. Add a little water from time to time to keep the meat juicy.

Carve the meat into slices, arrange on a hot plate, garnish with parsley and lemon. Serve with onion-fried potatoes.

(1 serving amounts to 601/2524 Cal/J)

Tip:

If you can not obtain a sac, wrap the prepared meat in aluminium foil and roast in the oven. Just before roasting is completed, remove the foil and let the meat roast some more until it turns golden brown.

Veal Scallop à la maître
(serves 4)

4 veal scallops
1 teaspoon Vegeta
60 g. (2 oz.) boiled smoked beef tongue
100 g. (4 oz.) fresh cottage cheese
1 teaspoon grated horseradish
salt, pepper
flour, eggs and bread crumbs for breading
frying oil

Thin out the scallops with a pounder. Slice the boiled tongue. Make the stuffing by mixing the well strained and mashed cottage cheese with grated horseradish, pepper and Vegeta.
Place 1-2 tongue slices on one half of the scallops, spread with the cheese mixture, cover with tongue slices. Cover with the other scallop half, season with salt, and beat the edges a little with a pounder so they join. Prepare the rest of the scallops in the same manner, cover with flour, dip into mixed eggs and bread crumbs.
Fry the scallops in hot oil until they turn golden-brown.
Serve with fried potatoes, risi-bisi (a rice and peas dish) and a salad of your choice.
(1 serving amounts to 478/2008 Cal/J)

Tip:

The scallops will be tender, juicy and golden-brown if you bread them just before frying. The frying oil must not be too hot because the scallops might overcook on the outside and become dry. But, if the frying oil temperature is too low, the scallops will absorb too much oil.

"Kramberger" Rolls
(serves 4)

600 g. (1.5 lb.) beef steak or steak fillet
Vegeta, 4 tablespoons oil
120 g. (4.5 oz.) thin smoked bacon slices
2 - 3 garlic cloves
200 g. (7 oz.) chopped tomatoes
1 teaspoon sugar
2 tablespoons cooked sour cherries from compote, 100 ml. (4 fl. oz.) red wine
parsley leaves
1 teaspoon breadcrumbs

Cut the meat into small slices and beat a little with a pounder. Spread crushed garlic over the slices, cover with bacon slices, roll up and fix with toothpicks. Fry the rolls briefly in hot oil, add chopped tomatoes and Vegeta. Simmer over a low heat until the meat becomes tender. Before it is almost cooked, add a little sugar, the sour cherries, wine and breadcrumbs to bind the

Scallop "Barun Trenk"

(serves 4)

600 g. leg of pork
aivar (red-pepper chutney), 40 g. (1.5 oz.)
kulen (paprika-flavoured salami)
1 hard-boiled egg, 4 tablespoon oil
200 g. (7 oz.) champignons (button mushrooms), salt, garlic
1 tablespoon Vegeta
2 tablespoons sour cream
wine to taste, hot red pepper
1 teaspoon cornflour, parsley

sauce. Salt and pepper to taste, sprinkle with chopped parsley and stir.

Serve with boiled rice or fried potato croquettes.

(1 serving amounts to 672/2822 Cal/J)

Tip:

If you use fillet steak for preparing this dish, less time will be needed for the meat to cook than if you use other beef cuts. Whichever meat you choose, it will be better if you cut the meat into slices, smear with oil and leave in a covered dish in the refrigerator, two to three days before preparing the dish.

Prepare four scallops, beat a little with a pounder, spread aivar over them. Place two thin slices of kulen on each and one fourth of egg on each scallop. Roll up the scallops and fix with toothpicks. Salt lightly and fry in oil on all sides. Add red pepper, braise adding water when needed, until the meat is tender. Take the scallops and the red pepper out of the pan and place them on a plate. Fry sliced champignons in the remaining oil, add chopped garlic, Vegeta and a little water. Place the rolls back into the pan and cook briefly. When they are almost cooked, add a little wine and sour cream to which you had added cornflour. Sprinkle with parsley.

Serve with boiled salted potatoes or mashed potatoes.

(1 serving amounts to 663/2785 Cal/J)

Skilful young cooks today present regional culinary customs and tastes in restaurants, applying new approaches in keeping up with modern world trends. Dishes often surprise us by name alone, while the ingredients are no less unusual: a combination of Slavonian kulen and fresh pork loin, sour cherries taken from compote together with beef steak or smoked beef tongue, fresh cottage cheese and ground horseradish with veal.

Pork Tenderloin Stubica Style

(serves 4-6)

There are dishes which have survived through the centuries. Pork Tenderloin Stubica Style is an unusual combination of ingredients, but typical Zagorje style, and legend has it that it dates as far back as the 16th century, when it was created in one of the numerous castles. At the end of the 20th century, leading Croatian chefs are winning over many gourmets and receiving awards with this superb dish.

2 pork tenderloins (about 800 g./1.75 lb. of fillet), 150 g. (5 oz.) prunes

4 tablespoons oil

30 g. (1 oz.) butter

1 tablespoon Vegeta

100 ml. (4 fl. oz.) sour cream

200 ml. (8 fl. oz.) fresh cream

150 ml. (5 fl. oz.) white wine

2 tablespoons slivovica (plum brandy)

salt, pepper, parsley

Wash and dry the meat. Make a cut through the centre of the meat. Pit the prunes and

put a speck of butter into each one. Place the pitted prunes side by side inside the meat. Some prunes will be left over. Salt and pepper the tenderloins and fry in hot oil on all sides. Add the rest of the pitted prunes cut into thin strips, Vegeta, and simmer over a low heat, adding wine and water when necessary. When the meat becomes tender, add the sour cream and fresh cream. Just before cooking is almost completed, add the slivovica.

Carve the meat into slices, arrange on a hot plate. Pour the roasting juices over the meat and sprinkle with chopped parsley. Serve with home-made flat noodles or rice.

(1 serving amounts to 827/3473 Cal/J)

Vineyard Pork Chops

(serves 4-6)

8 small pork chops
60 g. (2 oz.) prunes
150 g. (5 oz.) black grapes
30 g. (1 oz.) corn meal
60 g. (2 oz.) carrots
60 g. parsley root
20 g. (2/3 oz.) celeriac root
100 ml. (4 fl. oz.) red wine
2 tablespoons lard
1 tablespoon Vegeta
salt
pepper

Make a cut in the chop sides, salt and roll them in corn meal. Fry them in hot oil on both sides. Add the cleaned and diced root vegetables, pepper, and Vegeta and continue cooking over a medium heat, adding water when necessary. Add the stoned prunes and wine. When the chops are done, place them on a heated plate. Strain the sauce.

Pop the grapes into hot oil so the skin peels off easily. Add the grapes to the sauce. Boil briefly and pour over the chops.

Serve with home-made flat noodles.

(1 serving amounts to 536/2251 Cal/J)

Varaždin Feast

(serves 6)

600 g. (1.5 lb.) smoked pork half shank
600 g. (1.5 lb.) pork ribs
1 kg. (2 lb.) sauerkraut
50 g. (2 oz.) fat or lard
5 - 6 cloves garlic, salt, caraway seeds
1 tablespoon Vegeta

*T*raditional and nourishing meals tell us of the care taken in preparing food, and of the enjoyment in consuming it. Smoked meat with fatty parts combined with very healthy sauerkraut is favoured in Northwest Croatia where meat is marinated, cured, and where cabbage is pickled in wooden barrels, as it was in days long past.

Moisten the caraway seeds with a little water and chop finely. Mix with crushed garlic, salt and Vegeta. Rub part of this mixture into the pork ribs and leave the meat to rest for at least 1 hour.

Rinse the sauerkraut, especially if it is too sour. Boil the pork half shank briefly. Place the sauerkraut, the boiled pork half shank and the remaining garlic, caraway and Vegeta mixture into the pot. Add water and let it cook gently until everything becomes tender.

While the sauerkraut is cooking, place the prepared ribs to roast in the preheated oven. Baste with water during roasting as required. Carve the cooked half shank and the roast ribs into pieces. Arrange the sauerkraut on a heated plate, place the meat pieces on top.

(1 serving amounts to 905/3801 Cal/J)

Tip:

Serve polenta with this original Varaždin dish. According to an old custom in this part of the country, a combination of chopped bacon and ground pumpkin seeds is poured over the polenta.

Oxtail with Sauerkraut

(serves 4-6)

1 kg. (2 lb.) oxtail
8 tablespoons oil
80 g. (3 oz.) smoked bacon
150 g. (5 oz.) onions
150 g. carrots
10 g. (1/2 oz.) dry Boletus or other mushrooms
150 ml. (5 fl. oz.) red wine
Vegeta
2 bay leaves
1 kg. (2 lb.) sauerkraut
2 cloves garlic
salt
pepper

Cut the oxtail into pieces. Slice the bacon into small pieces. Heat the oil in a broad thick-based pan and fry part of the bacon. Add the oxtail, and fry well on all sides. Add the onion cut into quarters, and carrots sliced into thick slices. Salt lightly and stew. Add water occasionally, until the meat is half tender. Then add the bay leaf, coarsely ground pepper, chopped garlic, mushrooms previously soaked in a combination of water, Vegeta and wine. Cook briefly and arrange in an oven-proof casserole.

Cover with washed sauerkraut, the remaining bacon slices, and pour a little water over this. Put a cover on the casserole or wrap with aluminium foil. Bake in the oven for about 1 1/2 hour at 200°C/400°F/Gas Mark 6. Just before the end of cooking, uncover the casserole and bake uncovered until done.

Serve with boiled potatoes or white polenta.

(1 serving amounts to 824/3461 Cal/J)

Samobor Stew

(serves 5)

10 pork chops
1 pork half shank
2 tablespoon Vegeta
4 tablespoons lard
1/2 l. (20 fl. oz.) white wine
1 onion
salt, pepper
red paprika, hot pepper
sausages (garlic) as desired

A fair, a church feast or an excursion to the vineyard and wine-grower's hut at harvest or brandy making time can not have the right taste without meat prepared in the open in a wide, shallow platter with a wide rim. Each cook has his or her own secret as to the final taste of the meat - kotlovina. Citizens of Samobor can not be surpassed in this, thanks to their imagination and their daring in trying out new and unusual combinations.
It is different with wine goulash. Although beef and wine are always the main ingredients, it is prepared in hundreds of ways. It may be the plainest labourer's meal, but also served as a refined dish at celebrations, giving new energy after midnight.

Make cuts with a knife along the pork chops edges, and cut the half shank into pieces. Salt and leave to rest. Fry in hot oil together with onion slices. Place the fried meat on the platter edge, and fry the rest of the meat and sausages in the same manner.

Wine Goulash
(serves 4-6)

500 g. (18 oz.) beef
4 onions
60 g. (2 oz.) tomato puree
200 ml. (8 fl. oz.) wine
200 g. (7 oz.) potatoes
80 g. (3 oz.) pork fat or oil
salt
red paprika
bay leaf
caraway seed
1 tablespoon Vegeta

Replace the fried meat in the braising platter centre, add the hot pepper, pepper and Vegeta. Stew and add water when necessary, until the meat becomes tender. When the meat is almost cooked, add red paprika and pour the wine over the meat.

Serve with bean salad, pickled vegetables and good wine.

(1 serving amounts to 740/3108 Cal/J)

Note:

You may use other kinds of meat for *kotlovina*, such as neck of pork, chicken, and especially pork shank, which gives the sauce its characteristic taste and thickness.

Cube the meat and fry briefly in fat. Add chopped onions. Continue cooking, adding water or soup occasionally. Add the bay leaf, caraway seeds, and Vegeta. When it is almost cooked, salt to taste, add red paprika, tomatoes, wine and diced potatoes. Continue cooking until the potatoes and meat are tender.

(1 serving amounts to 444/1865 Cal/J)

Tip:

The more onions you use, the thicker the sauce will be. But, care must be taken that the onions do not burn, because then the goulash may taste bitter.

Pork Fillet with Lemon

(serves 4-6)

600 g. (1.5 lb.) pork fillet
50 ml. (2 fl. oz.) oil, 1 lemon
salt, white pepper, 10 g. (1/2 oz.) flour
100 ml. (4 fl. oz.) white wine
150 ml. (5 fl. oz.) fresh cream
20 g. (2/3 oz.) butter, parsley
1 tablespoon Vegeta

*S*callops are such a favourite dish that almost every town has its own scallop - "Viennese Scallop", "Paris Scallop", "Ljubljana Scallop".. The difference is in the type of meat used, the breading, and the stuffing. The scallop considered to be Zagreb style is a very tasty copy of the well known "cordon bleu" dish.

Cut the meat into small slices. Beat them with a kitchen pounder, rub in a little Vegeta and salt. Sprinkle with part of the lemon juice. Leave to rest a short while. Sprinkle with flour on one side. Fry in hot oil, firstly with the floured side down. When the meat turns golden-brown on both sides, pour

wine into the saucepan and stew slowly. When cooking is almost completed, add fresh cream, a little lemon juice, pepper to taste and add some more Vegeta.

If you wish to have a larger quantity of sauce, add some water and make it thicker by adding a teaspoon of cornflour. Cook briefly and add butter when almost cooked. Arrange the meat slices on a hot plate, pour sauce over them and garnish with peeled diced lemon rolled in chopped parsley.

Serve "ducats" or potato croquettes with this simple dish of refined taste.

(1 serving amounts to 541/2272 Cal/J)

Tip:

This recipe can be used to prepare veal fillet.

Sautéed Veal Scallop

(serves 4-5)

500 g. (18 oz.) veal leg
salt
flour
6 tablespoons oil

Cut the veal into scallops and cut each a little along the edge. Beat a little with meat pounder, salt and flour on one side only.

Fry the scallops, floured side down. When they are done on one side, turn and fry on the other side. Take them out and place on a hot plate. Add 3 - 4 tablespoons of water into the saucepan, bring to the boil, and pour over the scallops.

Serve the scallops with rice, mashed potatoes, or some other side dish.

(1 serving amounts to 373/1567 Cal/J)

Tip:

Pork scallops can be prepared in the same manner. They can be sprinkled with pepper or some chopped parsley.

Pork Chops Samobor Style

(serves 4-6)

| 8 pork chops (about 800 g./1.5 lb.) |
| 4 tablespoons oil |
| garlic, parsley, flour, salt |

*M*any people regard chops as the finest cuts of meat. However, the pleasure lies in the bone. In other words, the bone makes even fatty meat juicier and tastier, whether it is pork, veal or lamb. Pork chops are prepared in many various styles, according to the imagination of the cook. They may be grilled, breaded and fried, and marinated.

Beat the chops with a pounder, make cuts along the edges of each, salt and dust well with flour. Fry them in hot oil. After they have been fried for 5 -8 minutes on each side, sprinkle with chopped garlic. Place them on a hot platter. Pour a little water into the saucepan and let the sauce boil briefly. Pour the sauce over the fried chops. Serve with boiled potatoes sprinkled with parsley.

(1 serving amounts to 551/2314 Cal/J)

Pork Chops in Breadcrumbs with Horseradish

(serves 4-6)

8 pork chops (about 800 g. /1.5 lb.)
salt, pepper, 1 teaspoon Vegeta
60 g. (2 oz.) horseradish
50 ml. (2 fl. oz.) sour cream
eggs, flour and breadcrumbs
40 g. (1.5 oz.) butter
100 ml. (4 fl. oz.) frying oil

Make cuts along the pork chop edges with a knife, beat them with a pounder. Salt, sprinkle with Vegeta and freshly ground pepper. Mix grated horseradish with sour cream and a little salt, and spread the mixture over the pork chops. Then dip these chops into the whisked eggs, and cover with a breadcrumb and flour mixture.

Heat a mixture of oil and butter in a pan and fry the chops at moderate temperature on both sides. Take care that you first fry those sides which have the spreading. When the pork chops are golden, take them out and place on paper tissue to absorb the fat. Serve with fried potatoes and a fresh salad of your choice.

(1 serving amounts to 526/2209 Cal/J)

*S*ataraš (satarash) is a dish prepared from summer vegetables, primarily tomatoes, paprika and onion. The vegetables are diced with a special knife called a "satara". It is a very simple dish to prepare, but very refreshing and has a delicious taste.

Sataraš

(serves 4-6)

4 tablespoons oil
1 large onion
500 g. (18 oz.) paprika
400 g. (14 oz.) tomatoes
1 tablespoon sugar
salt
pepper
1 tablespoon Vegeta

Sauté the sliced onion in oil, add sugar, the peppers cut into small strips and continue cooking until the peppers have softened a little. Add peeled and diced tomatoes and Vegeta. Continue cooking until all the liquid evaporates. Add salt and pepper to taste.

(1 serving amounts to 133/559 Cal/J)

Tip:

Sataraš will be tastier if the peppers remain firm during sautéing. Using a wide saucepan will help the liquid evaporate as soon as possible.

Fried Pork Chops with Sataraš

(serves 4)

800 g. (1.5 lb.) pork chops
salt, pepper
sataraš

Cut the chops along the edges with a knife and beat them with a pounder. Sprinkle with a mixture of salt and pepper, brush with oil, and leave to rest for about 1 hour. Grill them or fry in a saucepan with a little oil. Serve with sataraš and boiled rice.

(1 serving amounts to 384/1613 Cal/J)

Fried Pork Chops with Champignons (Button mushrooms)

(serves 4)

8 small pork chops
salt, pepper
oil for frying
40 g./1.5 oz.) butter
200 g.(7 oz.) champignons (or other mushrooms)
1 clove garlic, parsley
100 ml. (4 fl. oz.) wine
100 ml. (4 fl. oz.) fresh cream
1 teaspoon cornflour
1 teaspoon Vegeta
hot pepper

Cut the pork chops along the edges and beat them with a pounder. Sprinkle with salt and pepper and fry in hot oil on both sides.

Fry the sliced mushrooms in heated butter in a separate pan. Add Vegeta, chopped garlic, a little hot pepper, and pour a mixture of wine and water into the pan. Cook briefly, and add the fresh cream mixed with cornflour.

Pour this sauce over the hot pork chops and sprinkle with chopped parsley.

Serve with flat noodles or potato croquettes.

(1 serving amounts to 635/2667 Cal/J)

Game and game dishes were not so rare in former times as they are today. Hunting grounds were easy to find and wild game dishes, as real delicacies, were an inspiration to writers and painters, as well as to cooks. Each region was specific for its wild game and for its recipes. Gorski Kotar was the region which made game dishes well known, and Baranja and Slavonija have their čobanac (chobanac - shepherd's stew) - meat stew often prepared with wild game. These dishes are prepared outdoors on an open spit or grill, or in a kettle, and have a very specific aroma. But they are no less tasty when prepared on the stove, in a pot. The recipes are often used to prepare other "ordinary" meat dishes, usually beef.

Hunter's Stew

(serves 4)

800 g. (1.5 lb.) venison or other wild game meat
400 g. (14. oz.) onion
bay leaf
salt, peppercorns
100 ml. (4 fl.oz.) white wine
50 ml. (2 fl.oz.) oil
1 tablespoon flour
1 tablespoon Vegeta
fried bread croutons

Dice the meat, fry in a little oil. Chop the onion roughly, and cook it in 2 l. (3.50 pints) slightly salted water with the peppercorns and a bay leaf. Simmer for about 30 minutes. Puree and add to the meat. Add Vegeta as well, cook slowly, until the meat is half-cooked. Add wine and a golden-brown roux, made from the remaining oil and flour. Cook for about 30 minutes more.

Serve as soup or a separate dish with boiled potatoes, fried bread croutons or small bread dumplings.

(1 serving amounts to 518/2176 Cal/J)

Venison Goulash with Prunes

(serves 4-6)

600 g. (1.5 lb.) venison, 200 ml. (12 fl. oz.) red wine, bay leaf, 4 allspice cloves
10 juniper berries, 200 g. (7 oz.) prunes
4 onions, 40 g. (1.5 oz.) smoked bacon
5 tablespoons oil, salt, pepper
500 ml. (20 fl.oz.) soup made from soup cube
200 ml. (8 fl.oz.) sour cream
100 ml. (4 fl.oz.) fresh cream

Put the bay leaf, allspice and crushed juniper berries into the wine. Pour this mixture over the stoned prunes and leave to soften for about half hour.

Cut the meat into small pieces. Fry in hot oil. When the meat is well browned on all sides, add finely chopped onion and bacon and continue cooking briefly. Season with salt and pepper to taste, cover and continue cooking, adding warm soup occasionally. When the meat is half cooked, add the prunes and about 100 ml. (4 fl. oz.) wine in which they had been soaked. Continue cooking until the meat is tender. Add the sour and fresh cream. Bring briefly to the boil.

Serve with home-made flat noodles.

(1 serving amounts to 509/2138 Cal/J)

Note:

Game goes well with sweet accompaniments. This is why game dishes are often served with sweet/sour tasting cranberries. Prunes taste better with venison goulash, and give the dish an even more distinctive taste.

Game Stew - Čobanac

(serves 4-6)

1kg. (2 lb.) game (venison, wild boar or the like)
2 onions, 2 garlic cloves
1 teaspoon ground hot paprika
1 teaspoon sweet paprika
2 bay leaves, 100 ml. (4 fl.oz.) tomato juice
1 tablespoon fat, salt, 100 ml. (4 fl.oz.)
wine, 1 tablespoon Vegeta

Cut the meat into small pieces and place in a saucepan with the chopped onions, bay leaf, fat, paprika, a little salt, Vegeta and enough water to cover the ingredients. Boil over a low heat until the meat is half tender. Add tomato juice, wine, chopped garlic.

Continue cooking until the meat is tender. The best indication that the čobanac is cooked is when we hear the bones "rustling" on the pot bottom when the pot is turned.

When everything is almost cooked, you can add flour dumplings or potato cubes to the čobanac, to taste. Sprinkle with parsley.

(1 serving amounts to 301/1264 Cal/J)

Braised Wild Duck

(serves 4)

1 wild duck	
salt, pepper	
Vegeta	
5 juniper berries	
4 tablespoons oil	
50 g. (2 oz.) smoked bacon	
1 carrot	
1 parsley root	
1 onion, bay leaf	
lemon rind	
200 ml. (8 fl. oz.) wine	
1 tablespoon flour	

*I*t was a must for hunters to exhibit lasting proof of their success - with trophies, horns and skins. But proof was often expressed by tasty dishes on a table around which there were men only. Dishes made from game are not as widely spread today as they were in times when hunting was considered an important branch of the economy, and when hunting was organised on hunting grounds, for the chosen few. However, recipes have been preserved and kept like the most precious trophies. Such is the case with the most frequent bag - birds such as wild duck or geese, quail, snipe, pidgeon...

Rub the cleaned duck well with a mixture of salt, pepper, Vegeta and crushed juniper berries. Leave to rest for about half an

hour. Place it in the roasting tin in hot oil and cover with bacon slices. Add diced carrot and parsley root, onion cut into big slices, bay leaf and a piece of thinly cut lemon rind. Bake in the oven. Baste with wine and water.

Carve the roast duck. Arrange on a hot plate, cover and keep warm. Dust the vegetables with flour, pour a little water over them, braise briefly and puree. Heat again, add salt to taste and pour this over the duck pieces.

Serve with potato croquettes, or bread dumplings.

(1 serving amounts to 685/2877 Cal/J)

Tip:

A little mild vinegar and a tablespoon of sugar can be added to the sauce.

Roast Pheasant

(serves 4)

1 pheasant
100 g. (4 oz.) smoked bacon
40 g. (1.5 oz.) butter
250 ml. (12 fl. oz.) white wine
200 ml. (8 fl. oz.) sour cream
salt
marjoram

Clean and wash the pheasant, rub with salt on the outside, and with marjoram on the inside. Cut the bacon into long, thin slices (fix with toothpicks, if necessary), and place on melted butter in a roasting tin. Roast at 200°- 220°C/400/Gas Mark 6/400°- 425°/Gas Mark 7. Baste with wine occasionally. When the pheasant becomes tender and golden-brown, pour sour cream over it and return to the oven to roast briefly.

Carve the roast pheasant into small pieces, so that each piece is covered with bacon. Pour roasting juices over them.

Serve with potato dumplings.

(1 serving amounts to 512/2150 Cal/J)

Venison à la compte

(serves 8-10)

2 kg. (4.5 lb.) leg of venison
Marinade:
1 tablespoon peppercorns
50 ml. (2 fl. oz.) wine vinegar
300 g. (11 oz.) carrots
150 g. (5 fl. oz.) parsley root
1 tablespoon cloves
1 tablespoon juniper berries
salt
Gravy:
100 g. (4 oz.) smoked bacon
150 g. (5 fl. oz.) fat
12 sugar cubes
rind of one lemon
40 g. (1.5 oz.) flour

Pour about 2 l. (3.5 pints) of water into a big saucepan. Add peppercorns, diced carrots, cloves, salt and juniper berries. Boil for about 15 - 20 minutes. Add vinegar and boil briefly. Leave the marinade to cool.

Wash the venison, place in the marinade and leave in a cool place. Turn the meat occasionally.

After 3 - 5 days, take the venison out of the marinade, season a little with salt, place in a roasting tin in the oven and roast. Baste with the marinade occasionally until the meat is tender. To prepare the sauce place the remaining fat in a big saucepan. When the fat is hot, first add the sliced bacon and then the sugar, and cook until brown. Mix with the vegetables from the marinade and cook until soft. Take the vegetables out of the pan, puree them and return into the sauce. Add roasting juices, flour and water mixture, lemon rind and cook briefly. When almost cooked, carve the meat into small pieces and place them in the sauce.

Serve with fried potato croquettes, fried mushrooms (champignons - button mushrooms), fried bacon slices and cranberries.

(1 serving amounts to 621/2608 Cal/J)

*T*he earliest traces of art show
how man was thankful for a good bag,
because this meant survival. Game was respected for its
beauty and for the skill needed in hunting it down. It was pres-
tigious to have luxurious hunting rooms, and to serve game
dishes in one's home, testimony to the great significance of hunting through the centuries. Croatia's hunting grounds today attract
sports' hunters from many countries who consider hunting a sport, hobby, and the source
of excellent gastronomic dishes.

odern fish-farms with big ponds and artificial-

ly fed fish remind us of the fish-ponds often

found near by Zagorje castles and mansions, which provided their

owners with sufficient fish during fasting periods. Fish such as

pike, perch, sturgeon, and carp were favourites because they were

easy to catch in the rivers and small backwater channels, rem-

nants of the ancient Pannonian Sea. A wooden boat, fishing net

and fishing kits were part of the landscape in regions like Posavi-

na, Podravina, Podunavlje, Pokuplje and other flatlands.

Breaded Sheat-fish or Carp
(serves 4)

8 sheat-fish or carp slices
salt
pepper
1 teaspoon red paprika
100 g. (4 oz.) maize flour
lemon, parsley
frying oil

Season the fish with salt and pepper, roll in
maize flour mixed with ground red paprika.

Fried Trout

(serves 4)

4 trout
lemon juice, salt, flour
frying oil, garlic
lemon
parsley

Heat the oil and fry the fish slices on both sides.

Serve on a heated plate with lemon slices.

Garnish with parsley.

Serve with potato salad or fried potatoes and fresh salad.

(1 serving amounts to 514/2159 Cal/J)

Clean, wash and dry the trout. Sprinkle with salt and lemon drops inside and out. Gently wipe with tissue. Roll the fish in flour and shake off the excess. Heat the oil and fry the fish. Arrange the fried trout on hot plates and garnish with lemon and parsley.

The trout may be prepared with chopped garlic and parsley mixed with oil. Serve with boiled or fried potatoes.

(1 serving amounts to 466/1957 Cal/J)

Fish Stew with Paprika (Čingi-lingi Stew)

(serves 4-6)

*C*arp is a catch for any fresh-water fisherman. Not always an easy one. But, in any case, carp can be found in many a stew or grill, cooked in the open air. Sometimes cured and fried afterwards. Sometimes breaded before frying.

1 kg. (2 lb.) various fresh-water fish
800 g. (1.5 lb.) onion
2 - 3 hot peppers
4 - 5 tablespoon oil
500 ml. (20 fl. oz.) white wine
bay leaf
parsley
salt
pepper
2 garlic cloves
30 g. (1 oz.) tomato puree
ground red paprika
a little flour
1 tablespoon Vegeta

Clean and wash the fish and cut off the heads and tails. Finely chop the onions and boil them with the fish heads and tails, and hot peppers. Simmer about 1 1/2 hours. Blend the ingredients and chill the soup stock.

Braise the remaining chopped onion, add garlic, tomato puree, and ground red paprika. Pour the chilled stock mixed with a little flour over the braised vegetables. Add the fish pieces, salt, pepper, and bay leaf. Salt to taste. Cook flat wide noodles in a separate saucepan and add to the stew just before serving. Sprinkle with chopped parsley.

(1 serving amounts to 405/1701 Cal/J).

Fried Carp

(serves 4)

1 kg (2 lb.) carp
1 tablespoon Vegeta
salt
30 g. (1 oz.) flour
6 tablespoons oil
1 kg. (2 lb.) potatoes
50 g. (2 oz.) bacon
2 - 3 pickled cucumbers
parsley
garlic
100 ml. (4 fl. oz.) white wine

Rub the cleaned carp with Vegeta. Roll in flour, place into hot oil in a covered baking tin, or cover with aluminium foil, and bake in the oven.

Pour a little oil into a separate saucepan, and briefly fry the bacon cut into small pieces and the diced potatoes. Add finely chopped cucumbers, chopped parsley and garlic to the fried potatoes, and mix. Arrange around the cooked carp. Pour wine over it, and cook briefly in the oven.

Serve the carp and potatoes with a salad of your choice.

(1 serving amounts to 522/2192 Cal/J)

Croatian Pancakes

(serves 4-6)

Batter:

250 g. (9 oz.) flour, 3 eggs
250 ml. (8 fl. oz.) milk, 250 ml. (8 fl. oz.)
mineral water, salt, frying oil

Filling:

400 g. (14 fl. oz.) fresh cottage cheese
3 eggs, 120 g. (4 oz.) sugar, lemon zest
300 ml. (1/2 pint) sour cream

*T*he greatest secret of tasty pancakes lies in their filling. The filling also determines whether they are going to be served as hors-d'oeuvres, the main dish or dessert. Croats like to have them with simple jam filling (rose hip jam and plum jam are the favourites). But when given the possibility to choose, the best-loved pancakes are with cottage cheese filling, baked in the oven (a Croatian variant), or pancakes with walnuts and wine chaudeau which may be found in other countries as well e.g. in Italy as zabaglione.

Mix the eggs with a pinch of salt in a deep bowl, adding flour, and milk and mineral water gradually. Bake the pancakes.
Cover pancakes with filling on one side only, without spreading, and roll them up. Arrange them in a buttered heat-resistant casserole and bake in the oven. Serve hot.
(one serving amounts to 249/1046 Cal/J)

Filling:

Mix the egg yolks and sugar until fluffy, add grated lemon zest, the strained cottage cheese, and the egg whites whisked into peaks. Fold in gently to get an even mixture.

Pancakes with Walnuts and Wine Chaudeau

(serves 4)

Batter
130 g. (4 1/2 oz.) flour
1 whole egg
1 egg yolk
250 ml. (12 fl. oz.) milk or mineral water
salt
frying oil
Filling:
80 g. (3 oz.) walnuts
20 g. (2/3 oz.) sugar
cinnamon
vanilla sugar
Wine chaudeau:
2 egg yolks
2 eggs
4 tablespoons sugar
30 ml. (10 fl. oz.) white wine

Mix the whole egg with the egg yolk, and a pinch of salt in a deep bowl. Gradually add flour and milk or mineral water. Bake the pancakes by taking a small ladle of batter and pouring it in the centre of the pancake pan on to the hot oil. Tip the pan so that the batter spreads evenly over the whole pan surface. When the underside is nicely brown, turn over the pancake and let it fry briefly. Fill the pancakes with a mixture of walnuts, cinnamon and vanilla sugar. Arrange them on a hot plate and top with wine chaudeau. Serve while still warm.

(1 serving amounts to 392/1646 Cal/J)

Wine chadeau:

Beat the egg yolks, eggs and sugar, add the wine and place into a steamer or bain Marie (in which the water is not quite boiling). Whisk until the mixture becomes a thick foam. Pour over the pancakes immediately.

*T*he name of a strudel usually depends on the filling. But whether the filling is prepared with cherries, sour cherries, apples, apples and walnuts, plums, poppy-seeds, rhubarb, cottage cheese, sultanas, raisins, hazelnuts and almonds..., whether prepared with proven dough, or thin pastry layers, the name strudel describes the manner of folding the filling. The word is of German origin and tells us that it is connected with Viennese cuisine, but it is also another term for the thin pastry called phyllo, coming to these parts originally with the Ottoman conquests. So the romantic connection between the two civilisations is found in the parchment thin, transparent drawn pastry.

Phyllo Pastry Strudels

Pastry:
300 g. (10 oz.) flour
2 tablespoons oil
100 - 200 ml (3 1/2 - 7 fl. oz.) lukewarm water, salt

Sift the flour on to a board, make a depression in the centre and put the oil in it. Mix by adding lukewarm salted water. When you have made a dough of soft consistency, knead it well with the hands or an electric blender until it is completely smooth. Divide the dough into two, brush with oil and leave it to stand for about 1/2 hour. Flour a tablecloth. Roll out the dough a little with a rolling pin, and then draw it out from the centre with floured fingers until it becomes almost transparent. Cut off the thick edges. Continue according to recipe for each individual strudel.

Plum Strudel

Filling:
1.5 kg (2 lb. 20 oz.) plums
150 g. (5 oz. butter)
50 - 70 g. (1 2/3 - 2 1/3 oz.) breadcrumbs
180 g. (8 oz.) walnuts
lemon zest, rum, cinnamon
100 - 150 g. (3 1/2 - 5 oz.) sugar
caster sugar for sprinkling

Sprinkle the drawn pastry with melted butter, then sprinkle two-thirds of the dough with fried bread crumbs, and arrange stoned and quartered plums on top. Sprinkle with roughly cut walnuts, grated lemon zest, cinnamon, sugar and rum. Roll up with the help of the tablecloth and place in a buttered tin. Brush the strudel with melted butter and bake for about 40 minutes at 200°C/ 400°F/ Gas Mark 6.

Sprinkle with sugar while still hot.

(1 serving amounts to 496/2083/J)

Apple Strudel

Filling:

1.5 kg (2 lb. 20 oz.) cooking apples, 120 g. (4 oz.) sugar, 80 g. (2 3/4 oz.) butter
50 - 70 g. (1 2/3 - 2 1/3 oz.) breadcrumbs
50 g. (1 2/3 oz.) sultanas or raisins
vanilla sugar, caster sugar for sprinkling

Peel the apples and grate them. Fry the breadcrumbs in butter and sprinkle over the drawn dough. Then sprinkle with grated apples, sultanas or raisins, sugar, vanilla sugar, cinnamon and rum. Roll up with the help of the tablecloth and place in a buttered tin. Brush the strudel with melted butter and bake for about 40 minutes at 200°C/ 400°F/ Gas Mark 6.

Sprinkle with sugar while still hot.

(1 serving amounts to 365/1533/J)

Sour Sherry Strudel

Filling:

50 g. (2 oz.) butter
700 g. (1.5 lb.) sour cherries, stoned
50 - 70 g. (1 2/3 - 2 1/3 oz.) breadcrumbs
150 g. (5 oz. sugar), cinnamon
vanilla sugar, butter for brushing
caster sugar for sprinkling

Fry the bread crumbs in butter, spread over the drawn dough. Arrange stoned sour cherries on top, sprinkle with sugar, vanilla sugar and cinnamon. Roll up with the help of the tablecloth and place in a buttered tin. Brush the strudel with melted butter and bake for about 40 minutes at 200°C/ 400°F/ Gas Mark 6.

Sprinkle with sugar while still hot.

(1 serving amounts to 308/1294/J).

*L*eavened-dough pastry has a really nostalgic aroma of past times when bread began its transformation into cake, and when the importance of dough leavening was discovered. Besides doughnuts, strudels or pies were the favourites. As dough kneading was a tough physical task, women competed in making these sweets. Everything was taken into consideration when determining whose pastry was best : the height, the softness, and how long the pastry stayed fresh. The filling thickness and richness evidenced the wealth of homes where the pastry was made. This dessert was a must at festive occasions.

Leavened-Dough Strudels/Rolls

Pastry:

30 g. (1 oz.) fresh yeast, 10 g. (2/3 oz.) sugar
50 ml. (2 fl. oz.) milk, 30 g. (1 oz.) flour
350 g. (12 oz.) flour, 50 g. (2 oz.) butter
30 g. (1 oz.) sugar, 2 egg yolks, 1 egg
200-300 ml. (8 fl. oz. - 10 fl. oz.) milk
1 tablespoon sour cream, lemon zest, rum
salt, egg for coating

Dissolve the sugar in a small amount of lukewarm water. Add flour, milk and crumbled yeast. Cover the bowl and allow the yeast to prove.

Place the flour in a warm bowl, add a pinch of salt, egg yolks and egg mixed with milk, melted butter, grated lemon zest, sour cream, rum and the proven yeast. Mix well and continue beating with a spoon or blend with a mixer until bubbles form.

Sprinkle a bowl with flour, place the dough into it, leave to prove until it doubles in size. Meanwhile mix the filling. Divide the risen dough into two, roll each half into a square the size of the baking tin. Spread filling over each half (cottage cheese filling, poppyseeds filling or walnut filling), and roll up. Place the rolls in a buttered baking tin, cover with a cloth and leave to prove some more. Preheat the oven, place the proven rolls inside and bake for 40 - 50 minutes at about 200°C/ 400°F/ Gas Mark 6.

When almost done, brush the rolls with the beaten egg.

Tip:

Dry yeast granules may be used instead of fresh yeast. It is not necessary to prove the dry granules. Mix the dry yeast granules with the flour and continue according to recipe.

Poppy Seed Roll (Makovnjača)

Filling:

300 g. (11 oz.) poppy seeds
250 ml. (8 fl. oz.) milk
150 g. (5 oz.) sugar
60 g. (2 oz.) sultanas or raisins
2 tablespoons rum, lemon zest, cinnamon

Grind the poppy seeds and scald them with hot milk. Soak the sultanas or raisins in rum. Mix the sultanas or raisins with the cool poppy seed mixture and add all the other ingredients.

(1 serving amounts to 518/2176/J).

Cottage Cheese Roll

Filling:

400 g. (14 oz.) fresh cottage cheese

2 eggs, 150 g. (5 oz.) sugar

50 g. (2 oz.) sultanas or raisins

lemon zest

1 sachet vanilla sugar

200 ml. (8 fl. oz.) sour cream

50 g. (2 oz.) butter

Mix the strained and creamed cottage cheese with egg yolk, sugar, sultanas or raisins, grated lemon zest, vanilla sugar and sour cream. Gently fold in the egg whites beaten to peaks.

(1 serving amounts to 451/1894/J)

Walnut Roll (Orehnjača)

Filling:

400 g. (14 oz.) walnuts

150 g. (5 oz.) sugar

100 g. (4 oz.) sultanas or raisins

200 ml. (8 fl. oz.) milk

2 tablespoons honey, lemon zest

cinnamon, 1 vanilla sugar

Grind the walnuts and scald with boiling milk. Wash the sultans or raisins and soak in rum. Combine the walnuts, sultanas or raisins, sugar, honey, vanilla sugar, cinnamon, lemon zest, and mix well.

(1 serving amounts to 631/2650/J)

Doughnuts

500 g. (1 lb.) flour	
1 sachet of dry yeast granules	
80 g. (2 3/4 oz.) butter	
40 g. (1 1/3 oz.) sugar	
100 - 150 ml. (3 1/2 fl. oz. - 7 fl. oz.) milk	
4 egg yolks	
2 tablespoons rum, lemon zest	
apricot jam, frying oil	
sugar for sprinkling	

*D*oughnuts are the most popular cakes deep-fried in oil. There was a time when this leavened dough was prepared mostly in winter, during heavy field work seasons, or at Carnival time when they were given to the masqueraders.

Today they are almost an everyday breakfast bought at the baker's. The most widely found doughnut is the one consisting of dough only, with or without a hole in the centre, sprinkled with caster sugar. But doughnuts with jam filling, and those with chocolate, vanilla or sugar topping are also popular.

Mix the yeast granules with flour. Whip the butter, sugar and egg yolks until fluffy. Add the grated lemon zest, rum, a small amount of milk, a little flour and season with salt. Continue mixing by adding the remaining milk and flour alternately. Make the dough smooth by beating it with a wooden spoon or in electric blender. Mix until the dough separates from the spoon and the sides of the bowl. Leave the dough to prove in a warm places until it doubles in size.

Roll out the proven dough until it is about 1/2 cm/1/4 inch thick, and cut out rounds with a glass that has a 8 cm/3.5 inch diameter or use a suitable tin mould. Coat the edges of the rounds with egg whites, and put a small quantity of jam in the centre of each, cover with another dough round and trim edges with a small glass or mould. Arrange the doughnuts on a floured board and leave to prove covered with a cloth. Place the proven doughnuts in a large quantity of hot oil with the upper side down. Fry, covered, for about three minutes. Turn them over and continue cooking uncovered until the other side also turns golden brown. Take them out of the frying pan with a slotted spoon and place on oil absorbing tissue. Sprinkle with sugar while still hot.

(1 serving amounts to 353/1483/J).

Tip:

You can prepare the doughnuts in a more simple way. Make a round out of a thick layer of rolled out proven dough, let it prove and fry in oil. Fill the cool doughnuts with jam, or, more simply, serve the jam with the doughnuts.

Gugelhupf

400 g. (14 oz.) flour
1 packet dried yeast granules
80 g. (2 3/4 oz.) butter
40 g. (1 1/3 oz.) sugar
3 egg yolks
lemon zest
salt
rum
vanilla sugar
50 g. (1 3/4 oz.) sultanas or raisins
200 ml (7 fl oz.) milk
sugar for sprinkling

Mix the yeast granules with flour. Whip the butter, sugar and egg yolks until fluffy. Add the flour and milk alternately, and the grated lemon zest, salt, rum, vanilla sugar and sultanas or raisins. Mix well. Place the prepared mixture into a buttered and floured gugelhupf mould, cover it and leave to prove in a warm place. Preheat the oven, bake for about 50 minutes at 200°C /400°F/ Gas Mark 6. Take the cake out of the mould, put it on a plate and sprinkle with caster sugar.

Tip:

To check whether the gugelhupf is done, pierce it lightly with a skewer. If the skewer comes out clean and dry, the cake is baked.

*T*here was a time when gugelhupf was a must together with Sunday morning coffee with milk, the same way as a trip to the country was a must for well-to-do town families. The explanation is in the time-consuming preparation. This round cake is baked in various moulds, which may be made of various materials, and there are still doubts about its name, although it probably comes from the word Kugel, which is a word describing a type of hill in the Alps, or from Gugel, which means a high object, or a hat fashionable in the 12th century. Hupf or Hopf probably associates jumping with the dough rising, and this is why this cake with ancient roots has the Croatian name "naduvak".

Bishop's Bread

| 140 g. (5 oz.) sugar, 4 eggs, orange rind |
| 50 g. (2 oz.) walnuts or almonds |
| 100 g. (4 oz.) raisins or sultanas |
| 50 g. (2 oz.) chocolate |
| 140 g. (5 oz.) flour, sugar for sprinkling |

Mix sugar and egg yolks until fluffy. Add grated orange rind, walnuts or almonds cut into flakes, raisins or sultanas, diced chocolate. Mix well and alternately add flour and egg whites beaten to the stiff peak stage. Fold in gently and pour into a floured and buttered mould (30 x 10 cm / 12 x 4 inches). Bake about 40 minutes at 190°C/375°F /Gas Mark 5. Remove the cake from the mould. Sprinkle with caster sugar.
(1 serving amounts to 234/983/J)

Walnut Pie

Pastry:
300 g. (10 oz. flour)
250 g. (9 oz.) butter or margarine
50 g. (1 2/3 oz) sugar, one egg
1 tablespoon sour cream, salt

Filling:
8 eggs, 300 g. (10 oz.) sugar
300 g. (10 oz.) walnuts
10 g. (4 oz.) sultanas or raisins
cinnamon, nutmeg, rum, lemon zest
sugar for sprinkling

Make a dough out of the flour, butter, sugar, eggs, sour cream and a pinch of salt, and set aside, covered, in a cool place. Roll out the dough into two pieces (one bigger in size) in accordance with the tin size (approx. 35 x 20 cm/14 x 8 inch). Put the larger dough piece into the buttered tin so that the edges are raised upwards. Pour in the walnut filling. Cover with the other piece of dough. Before baking, pierce the upper layer of pastry with a fork. Bake for about 50 minutes at 200°C/425 °F / Gas Mark 7. While still hot, sprinkle the baked pie with sugar. When it has cooled, cut into squares. (1 serving amounts to 615/2583/J)

Filling:
Mix the egg yolks and sugar until fluffy, add the ground walnuts, sultanas or raisins soaked in rum, cinnamon, some grated nutmeg, grated lemon zest, then gently fold in the egg whites beaten to the stiff peak stage.

Tip:
Instead of a square tin you may use a round form to bake this pie in, and serve it as a cake.

Apple Pie

Pastry:
400 g. (14 oz.) flour
300 g. (10 oz.) butter or margarine
70 g. (2 1/3 oz.) sugar, 2 egg yolks
2 tablespoons sour cream, a pinch of salt

Filling:
150 g. (5 oz.) apricot jam
1 kg (2 lb. apples), 60 - 80 g. (2 - 2 3/4 oz.) sugar, cinnamon, vanilla sugar, 50 g. (1 2/3 oz.) sultanas or raisins, sugar for sprinkling

Rub the flour and the chilled butter cut into flakes into crumb consistency, add the sugar, egg yolks, sour cream and a pinch of salt. Knead into a dough. Set aside to rest for 1 - 2 hours. Divide the dough into two portions and roll them out. Place one portion into a tin dusted with flour (about 40 x 25 cm/16 x 10 inch in size) and bake. Spread jam and filling over the half-baked pastry, cover with the other portion of dough, pierce with a fork, and continue baking at 200°C/400°F/ Gas Mark 6, until done. Sprinkle sugar over the hot pie and cut into squares. (1 serving amounts to 380/1596/J)

Filling:
Slice the peeled apples into small pieces. Add sugar, cinnamon, vanilla sugar, lemon juice and braise briefly. Add the sultanas or raisins.

Cottage Cheese Pie

Pastry:

300 g. (10 oz. flour)
pinch of baking powder
200 g. (7 oz.) butter
100 g. (3 1/2 oz.) sugar
2 egg yolks
1 tablespoon sour cream
lemon zest
a pinch of salt

Filling:

4 egg whites
200 g. (7 oz.) sugar
500 g. (1 lb. 1 2/3 oz.) fresh cottage cheese
lemon zest
vanilla sugar
100 g. (3 1/2 oz.) sultanas or raisins
sugar for sprinkling

Mix the baking powder with the flour. Crumb this with the butter cut into flakes.

Add sugar, egg yolks, grated lemon zest, sour cream and a pinch of salt. Knead the shortcake dough, then set aside for a short while. Roll out the dough into two pieces, one of which should be larger than the other and placed into a buttered baking tin (approx. 30 x 20 cm/12 x 8 inch in size). Spread the filling on this layer and cover with the other piece of dough, pierce with a fork, and bake at 200°C/ 400°F/Gas Mark 6 for about 50 minutes.

Sprinkle sugar over the hot pie and cut into squares.

(1 serving amounts to 498/2092/J)

Filling:

Whisk the egg whites to the stiff peak stage, then add sugar gradually at the end. Add the strained creamed cheese, washed sultanas or raisins, grated lemon zest and vanilla sugar, and fold in gently.

Tip:

Add a tablespoon of semolina if the filling is too soft because the cheese is too fresh.

Chestnut Cake

Pastry:
70 g. (2 1/3 oz.) butter, 150 g. (5 oz.) sugar
5 eggs, 70 g. (2 1/3 oz.) flour
1/2 teaspoon baking powder, 30 g. (1 oz.)
bread crumbs, 100 g. (4 oz.) chocolate

Filling:
350 g. (12 oz.) chestnut puree, 50 g. caster
sugar, 3 - 4 tablespoons ground walnuts
a few drops of rum, 1 sachet vanilla sugar
400 ml. (16 fl. oz.) double cream
6 gelatine sheets

Icing:
100 g. (4 oz.) chocolate
20 tablespoons caster sugar
3 tablespoons water, 80 g. (3 oz.) butter

Mix the butter and sugar until fluffy, blend in the egg yolks. Gradually add the flour mixed with the baking powder. Add bread crumbs, and the softened chocolate. Fold in gently egg whites beaten to stiff peak stage. Pour the mixture into a buttered cake tin sprinkled with bread crumbs. Bake for about 30 minutes at 180°C/350°F/Gas Mark 4. When the cake is cool, cut it into three equal layers. Sprinkle a little milk over one layer, spread half the filling over it, cover with the second layer and repeat the procedure. Top the cake with warm chocolate icing.
(1 serving amounts to 254/1067/J)

Filling:
Mix the sugar, vanilla sugar, rum and walnuts into the chestnut puree. Then blend in the double cream with the gelatine.

Icing:
Melt the chocolate mixed with water and sugar by gently heating over steam until the mixture becomes smooth. While still hot, gradually blend in the butter cut into flakes.

Old-fashioned Pepper Biscuits

750 g. (1.75 lb.) flour
370 g. (13 oz.) ground walnuts
120 g. (4 1/2 oz.) sugar
500 g. (18 oz.) honey (locust flower if available), 180 g. (6 oz.) rendered butter
3 egg yolks
1 lemon
cinnamon, a clove
3 tablespoons white pepper
egg yolk and water for coating

Bring the honey to the boil, add sugar and butter, continue cooking and stirring until all the ingredients melt. Leave to cool. Sift the flour and mix well with ground walnuts, grated lemon zest and spices. Make a well in the flour. Place the egg yolks in this well and mix gradually with the flour. Gradually add the honey mixture and make a dough. Make several balls out of the dough and leave to rest, preferably in a cool place, overnight.
Make the pepper biscuits the following day with a special wooden mould. Cut a piece of dough into pieces, and form a thick roll out of each piece. Place the roll on the floured mould, press it into the mould firmly, and flatten out the dough surface. Turn the mould and press it over a flat surface. Cut off surplus dough around the mould and lift the mould. Place the pepper biscuits in a buttered tin and bake at 180°C/ 350°F/ Gas Mark 4.
(1 serving amounts to 435/1827/J)

Note:
For tasty pepper biscuits the most important thing is to balance well the listed spices so that no one spice prevails. If you do not have a pepper biscuit mould, the biscuits can be cut out with a decorative wheel.

Tip:
If you do not have rendered butter, melt and cook ordinary butter, ladle off the foam from its surface and keep refrigerated until used.

Honey Biscuits

350 g. 12 oz. flour
1/4 sachet baking powder
150 g. (5 oz.) butter, 200 g. (7 oz.) sugar
2 eggs, 2 tablespoons rum (or brandy)
100 g. walnuts or almonds
1 tablespoon cinnamon
2-3 tablespoons honey, nutmeg, lemon zest
egg white for coating

Mix the baking soda evenly with the flour, crumb together with butter cut into pieces. Add the sugar, eggs, rum, ground walnuts or almonds, cinnamon, honey, ground nutmeg, ground lemon zest and knead well. Keep in a cool place for at least one hour or overnight. Then make rolls and cut them into equal pieces, the size of a walnut. Form into balls, arrange in a buttered pan, flatten slightly, decorate with walnut or almond pieces, and brush with the egg white.
Bake for about 15 minutes at 220°C°/425°F /Gas Mark 7.

Bear Paw Cookies

3 cups flour, 1/4 sachet baking powder

1 cup sugar, 2 cups ground walnuts

1 cup lard

1 egg, 1-2 tablespoons honey

1 sachet vanilla sugar, caster sugar

Mix the ground walnuts with the flour, baking soda and sugar. Make a well in the centre, put in the whole egg, honey, softened lard, vanilla sugar, and make a dough. Leave about 30 minutes in a cool place. Coat tin moulds (the shape of bear paws) with lard, powder with flour, and fill with the prepared dough, but not to the top. Press gently so that the form comes out clearly. Put the moulds with the dough into a baking tin and bake for about 20 minutes at 220°C/ 425°F /Gas Mark 7, until the dough browns. While still hot, take the bear paws out of the moulds and roll in caster sugar.

(1 serving amounts to 197/827/J)

*H*oney biscuits with pepper i.e. pepper biscuits, are proof of how new spices were included in our meals. These biscuits are probably the only sweets including pepper. Having discovered new spices, and having the means to buy them and use them, people living in this country used them at random. Pepper biscuits are aromatic Christmas sweets, and require skill and time to make because they are made with wooden moulds as in olden times, and they are imprinted with symbols such as a fish, lamb, cock or a cross, which link paganism and Christianity.

Mediterranean Cuisine

*C*roatian cuisine along the coast, on the Adriatic islands, and in the hinterland is typically Mediterranean, following the principles of modern nutritional trends. Short cooking time, plenty of fish, vegetables and olive oil are its main characteristics. Such cooking is healthy and also very tasty and has many variants. The Istrian peninsula alone has two specific cuisines : that along the coast and that inland. The regions of Gorski Kotar, Lika, Dalmatinska Zagora, Imotska Krajina and further into Herzegovina are separated from the Primorje and Dalmatian cuisine by the highest and most rugged Croatian mountains, only to come together finally in "Croatian California", the rich and fertile river Neretva valley through the Pelješac peninsula on to the magic world of the islands.

*H*istory is very much alive in this cuisine. When ordering meat cooked under a peka one does not realise how close one is to the Illyrian world of 3000 thousand years ago. When inhabitants of the island of Vis roast fish over a spit rather than in the usual manner on a grill, they do it just as the old Greeks and Romans once did on their island, then called Issa. The round unleavened flat buns prepared on the island and served with pilchards resembles archaeological layers, and if prepared without tomatoes date from before Columbus's discovery of America. On the other hand, if tomatoes are added, they date from the times when Columbus's vessels had already brought tomatoes to Europe. More recent times dating back no more than five centuries, are found in the aromas: even in the town of Šibenik which was never reached by the Turks, Arambašići (stuffed sauerkraut rolls) are prepared with oriental spices. Excellent prosciutto (Parma ham) goat cheese, pasta (spaghetti, noodles, farfalle), sauces and various manestras (the green soup from Dubrovnik, Istrian soups which depend on the seasonal vegetables) are next of kin to another Mediterranean cuisine - that of Italy, while the simple fish soup "bujabež" (bouillabaisse) is a first cousin to the best French cooking. And there is even traditional truffle harvesting in Istria.

*G*ood food and good wines have always inspired artists. Croatian literature would be poorer had not Ribanje i ribarsko prigovaranje (Fishing and Fishermen's Conversation) been written by Petar Hektorović in the 16th century, describing a three-day fishing trip with two fishermen, Paskoje and Nikola, from the island of Hvar. Among snippets of folk wisdom, fishing, the sea and fishing nets are discussed. The comedy Dundo Maroje, written by the Dubrovnik writer Marin Držić, is a Renaissance work glorifying various forms of pleasure through the character of Dugi Nos. Pomet compares the Dubrovnik tables with those of Rome, naming the food seen in three hours as "gvacet" which could bring the dead back to life: cabbage soup, German bacon, muštarda (mustard), a chicken platter, a plump duck, two quails, a pheasant, a goose .. And he shouts: "We are among delicacies, we are in Heaven!". In our century a part of these wonders can be found in the recipes written by Dika Marjanović Radica and contained in her book Dalmatinska kuhinja (Dalmatian Cuisine).

The Mediterranean gives generously of itself in its Croatian part as well. Fish and fruits of the sea, sheep and goats, vineyards and wine, exclusively wine vinegar, fresh and dried grapes, grape brandy, figs, olives and olive oil, boiled or grilled meat, cultivated and wild growing vegetables, aromas and spices are all the true stamp of this modern cuisine. Inhabitants of Blato on the Island of Korčula or of Murter in the Kornati islands have no trouble finding as many as some forty wild growing edible plants and herbs in the rocks and macchia which grow in particular places. Herb-flavoured brandy is famous mostly for its green ingredients. The Lika cuisine is also very good for one's health although it is extremely plain : boiled lamb, fermented cheese (škripavac, basa), maize polenta. One of its specialities is young lamb with sour sheep milk.

In those parts the hearth, called the komin, was the centre of the home. Bread was baked and young lamb or goat was roasted under a peka, while all meals were prepared in the same kettle - polenta, boiled meat, pasta, manestra. Even prosciutto (Parma ham) and cheese were first dried over the hearth, and then in the north wind, the bura, or in the sun. Pag island cheese and Pag lamb do not need to be seasoned with salt. The pastures provide all the necessary salt, helped by the Velebit bura. In other places cheese and fish were kept in salt : a row of fish and a row of salt alternately. Cheese and fish were also conserved covered with olive oil. Olives and capers are sometimes conserved in a salt brine or they are baked in the oven, always after having been previously soaked in sea-water. In every home these foodstuffs are a must. But no home can be without a konoba - a cool storage place, and, often, a cool venue for drinking wine with friends.

The Karst regions were rough places to travel through, and experience was exchanged slowly. Habits changed faster in those places where ships arrived with tales and foodstuffs from all over the world. Maybe this is how rose water came to Croatia, used as one of the ingredients when making rožata, a type of baked custard, or pinca, a sweet bread loaf. The most specific cuisine is found on the most distant islands such as Vis, Hvar, Brač, Korčula, Pag, Krk, Rab. People there could survive on what they grew themselves and could also export their products.

If you visit the Mediterranean part of Croatia, do not pass through without tasting Dalmatian and Istrian prosciutto (Parma ham), Pag cheese, cheese preserved in oil, Lika cheeses, basa and škripavac, green and black olives, pickled onions, asparagus and artichokes, or a wild herb mixture, at least one of the pastas, Istrian stew called jota, arambašići rolls, lamb baked under a peka, boiled lamb, octopus salad and sailor's risotto. Scampi, shells and crabs are a delicacy, no matter how they are prepared. Fried fish are as well. If you do not taste a dentex, gilthead or sea-bass, only gently grilled or boiled with the addition of a red scorpionfish or so, it would be as if you had not visited the Adriatic coast. Brodetto (fish soup) and buzara (a dish made from shells) are a must, the same as pašticada (beef dish) with gnocchi (potato dumplings), or as cod prepared at Christmas and Easter fasting. Fritters, pinca (sweet loaf), rožata (egg pudding), paradižet, Hvar pepper cookies, rafioli (fritters), fig cake are sweets which have been prepared in southern Croatia for centuries, and have always been offered as a welcome to dear guests. You will not make a mistake even when you try stone soup!

Cold hors d'oeuvres

There is no greater pleasure than to go down to the konoba, take a prosciutto (Parma ham) dried in the bura wind, and slice it to be as thin as paper. In Istria they will praise its softness and pleasant pink colour, while on the islands of Dalmatia, and in Drniš, they will praise its rosiness and toughness. The dark coolness of the konoba also preserves cheese, pilchards in salt and oil, pickled onions, raisins and dried figs. Black and green olives still have the aroma of the sea in which they are soaked before being arranged in glass bottles and filled with salted brine, or baked in the oven to last longer. If nothing else, there was always thick olive oil in which black bread or unleavened flat buns could be dunked. And wine, black and heavy. There is always a pitcher, the traditional wooden bokaleta, beside the wine barrel in the kono-

ba. The Istrians have made a special refreshment from God's bounty for winter night companionship: teran borgonja or white wines are heated by the fire, flavoured with sugar, pepper and a few drops of olive oil, and toasted bread is added to this "soup". The bokaleta is passed around the circle of friends, to the exchange of various stories. Perhaps the finest thing passed around is the cheese, sheep milk cheeses primarily. In Lika smoked cheese is offered, the Pag cheese on the island of Pag, which was dried and salted in the air, flavoured by the rare herbs the sheep fed on along the rocks. Further towards the south, as in Dubrovnik and on the islands, cheese is stored in oil with aromatic herbs. In Metković, Imotski and Dalmatinska Zagora towards Herzegovina, cheese is dried and stored in goatskin.

The traditional cold hors d'oeuvres of the Mediterranean hinterland are very simple to make. But the secret of the long life of mountain inhabitants may lie in the food prepared in various parts along the Velebit, Risnjak, Dinaric, and Biokovo mountain ranges where the two climates meet : the Mediterranean and the continental. Potato halves baked in the oven all the year round, sauerkraut during the long winters, spring onions from spring till autumn, maize flour bread, and even prosciutto made from bear meat tell of the care taken in Lika and Gorski Kotar in respect to food. Provision had to be made for the long winters and the possibility of barren years. There is no better example than with cheese. Sour milk and fermented cheeses are especially appreciated in Lika: basa, a very soft cheese made from cooked, skimmed and soured milk, and the fatty and salted škripavac made from cow and sheep milk.

Gorski Kotar Stuffing

(serves 10)

300 g. (11 oz.) ham or fatty pork neck
100 g. (4 oz.) dried bacon
15 eggs
1 bunch of spring onions (green parts)
200 g. (7 oz.) bread without crust
salt, freshly ground pepper

Add chopped onions, ham, bacon and bread diced into small pieces to the mixed eggs. Season with pepper, blend well and add salt, if necessary.

Fill a buttered rectangular mould with this mixture. Cover with foil and place into a bigger tin filled with hot water. Bake for about 1 hour in the oven at 220°C/425 F°/Gas Mark 7.

Shake the baked stuffing out of the mould, chill and cut into slices. Arrange on a plate together with ground horseradish, ham, škripavac cheese and spring onions.

(1 serving amounts to 363/1525 Cal/J).

Note:

This is a modern, simple variant of the dish from Gorski Kotar. In past times the prepared mixture was stuffed into a pork stomach, smoke-dried and then cooked, usually at Easter when many other dishes containing a large quantity of eggs were prepared with various additions. Usually it was served with ham and spring onions.

Beef Soup

(serves 4-6)

600 - 800 g. (1.5 - 1.75 lb.) beef
1.5 l (2 pints) water
1 bunch root vegetables
1 - 2 tomatoes, 2 potatoes
1 onion
1 cabbage leaf
peppercorns
salt, Vegeta
celeriac leaf

Pour lukewarm water into a pot and place the meat in it. As soon as the soup comes to the boil, add the cleaned root vegetables (celeriac, carrots, and parsley), several peppercorns, and the onion previously cut into halves and scorched on the stove plate. Then add tomatoes, peeled potatoes, the cabbage leaf, Vegeta and celery leaf, and cover the pot. When the soup comes to the boil again, lower the heat, and simmer slowly for about two hours. When the meat is cooked, add some cold water so that the soup becomes clear.

Take the meat out of the soup, and strain the soup through a fine sieve. Cook some rice or pasta in the soup.

(1 serving amounts to 119/500 Cal/J)

Lamb Soup

(serves 6)

300 g. (11 oz.) cured meat or prosciutto
(Parma ham)
500 g. (18 oz.) lamb or mutton
1 large carrot
a piece of celeriac root
2 small tomatoes
1 small onion
1 small garlic clove
celery leaf
parsley leaf
salt, peppercorns

Wash the cured meat well, boil briefly, drain it and place in fresh water to cook some more. When it is half cooked, add the lamb, salt, peppercorns, onion, garlic clove, the carrot and tomato cut in halves, celery and parsley leaves. Continue cooking for about one more hour. When the meat is tender, take it out of the soup. Strain the soup. You can cook some pasta (small noodles) or rice in the strained soup.

While the soup is cooking, you can add a cabbage leaf or two, and 1 - 2 potatoes. (1 serving amounts to 234/983 Cal/J)

Even those who do not know much about Croatian cuisine will notice how popular various soups are. But only the connoisseur will be able to tell the differences in the preparation. In southern Croatia beef is used in soup more often than chicken, and tomatoes are also added. Even the clearest Dalmatian soups are strong and aromatic. Rice, or various pasta, are usually cooked in the soup when it is almost done. Noodles or dumplings are rarely added, whereas they are a must in northern Croatia.

If a meal consists of several courses, meat and vegetables cooked in the soup will be the course following the soup, together with boiled potatoes and the very popular tomato sauce - salsa - based on ripe red tomatoes, garlic, onion and olive oil, providing a wonderful and authentic taste of the south.

If the meal is planned to be a simple one, especially if it is based on a prosciutto (Parma ham) bone, lamb head or dried mutton, the soup will be thickened by addition of various vegetables, making it a substantial meal in itself.

Artichokes With Peas

(serves 4)

8 artichokes
lemon juice, 4 tablespoons breadcrumbs
100 ml. (4 fl. oz.) olive oil, 4 cloves garlic
parsley, salt, pepper, 50 g. (2 oz.) shelled
peas, 1 tablespoon Vegeta

Clean the artichokes, remove the tough leaves, cut off the hard stalks and the sharp leaf ends. Boil briefly in salted water with a little lemon juice, and then drain. Mix the bread crumbs, chopped garlic, parsley, pepper and Vegeta. Spread the artichoke leaves and spoon the mixture between the leaves. Put the peas in a saucepan. Arrange the artichokes on top, heads up. Pour in the oil, season with a little salt and pour cold water over them so they are completely covered. Cook over a low heat for about an hour and a half. When most of the liquid evaporates, add a little more oil.

The artichokes may be prepared with young broad-beans instead of peas.

(1 serving amounts to 327/1373 Cal/J)

Two green vegetables, growing wild or cultivated, are a favourite on the Croatian table. Artichokes were grown particularly in central Dalmatia, around the towns of Zadar and Split. They were considered a delicacy, even when only boiled and seasoned. There are bitter liqueurs and medicines based on artichokes. Growing wild, asparagus is found along the whole Adriatic coastline. Istria has made up its own culinary tale based on asparagus, by preparing it with eggs. Fried eggs with various additions have been a favourite in all periods all over the world, but Istrian fritajas and fritadas are special because they have the aroma of prosciutto (Parma ham), bacon, truffles...

The same softness is characteristic for sauces to which asparagus and other wild growing herbs are added. These are most often only cooked and seasoned, so as not to lose their specific taste.

Boiled Artichokes

(serves 4)

8 artichokes, lemon juice
peppercorns, 50 g. (2 oz.) olive oil
Sauce:
1 teaspoon mustard
4 teaspoons wine vinegar
80 ml. (3 fl. oz.) olive oil, 1 teaspoon sugar
2 cloves garlic, parsley, salt, pepper

Wash the artichokes, clean the leaves, cut off the hard stalks and the sharp ends of the remaining leaves. Boil briefly in salted water with a little lemon juice added. Drain, spread the leaves out a little, and arrange side by side in a saucepan, so they stand head up. Pour the oil over them, season with salt, add freshly ground pepper and cover them completely with cold water. Allow to simmer about and hour and a half. The water should evaporate completely, so in the end they cook in their own juices and the oil.

Serve sauce with the boiled artichokes. Prepare the sauce by mixing a teaspoon of mustard with wine vinegar, adding olive oil gradually, and finally a little sugar. Also add chopped parsley and garlic, salt and pepper.

If liked, chopped chives and capers can be added.

(1 serving amounts to 305/1281 Cal/J)

Fritaja with Asparagus

(serves 4-6)

4 bunches wild asparagus
6 eggs, 1 onion
50 g. (2 oz.) olive oil
salt, pepper

Wash the asparagus, remove the hard parts leaving the soft stalks and tops. Break into small pieces. Briefly fry finely chopped onion in oil, add the asparagus pieces, season with salt and pepper. Cook until the asparagus is tender. Add mixed eggs, stir gently and cook until done.

(1 serving amounts to 180/756 Cal/J)

Boiled Wild Asparagus

(serves 4-6)

4 bunches wild asparagus (about 500 g./18 oz.)
6 eggs, 50 ml. (2 oz.) olive oil
salt, pepper

Clean the asparagus, discarding the hard parts. Wash the soft stalks and tops and cook in a little water. Season with salt. When they are tender, drain, season with pepper and sprinkle with oil. Arrange on a plate with hard-boiled eggs.

(1 serving amounts to 179/752 Cal/J)

Spaghetti with Meat Sauce
(serves 4-6)

400 g. (14 oz.) spaghetti, salt
Sauce:
50 ml. ((2 fl. oz.) olive oil and sunflower oil mixture, 250 g. (9 oz.) minced veal
50 g. (2 oz.) smoked bacon (or prosciutto (Parma ham), 1 onion, salt, peppercorns
1 carrot, 20 g. (2/3 oz.) celeriac root
20 g. (2/3 oz.) tomato or 2 tablespoons tomato puree, 2 cloves garlic, nutmeg
2 cloves, 100 ml. (4 fl. oz.) white wine grated sheep cheese

*T*he whole Mediterranean area is very fond of good pasta, and the Croatian coast is no exception. Italian neighbours have used their imagination and have become the first in turning pasta, as well as pizza, into international foods, popular all over the world. Croatians have excellent pasta, but tend to be very traditional in preparing it. Here we present traditional pasta dishes with sauces, but almost any pasta may be combined with any sauce.

Heat the oil in a saucepan and fry the minced meat. Add the bacon or prosciutto (Parma ham) cut into small pieces, onion and garlic, then the grated carrot and celeriac root, cook some more. Add the tomato cut into small pieces (previously peeled and cleaned of seeds), salt, grated nutmeg and cloves. Mix well, pour in the wine and simmer slowly for about an hour, adding water if necessary. Season the cooked sauce with pepper to taste, mix with the cooked and strained spaghetti. Sprinkle with grated cheese.
(1 serving amounts to 469/1970 Cal/J)

Pasta Shells with Tomato

(serves 4-6)

350 g. (12 oz.) pasta

50 g. (2 oz.) fresh tomato or canned whole
tomatoes, 50 ml. (2 fl. oz.) olive oil

2 cloves garlic, salt, pepper

a little sugar if desired, parsley, Vegeta

Briefly fry a little sugar in the heated olive oil together with finely chopped garlic and half of the parsley (chopped). Remove the skin and seeds from the tomato, and add the tomato slices to the pan. Season with a little salt and pepper. Add Vegeta and simmer over a low heat for about 30 minutes. When cooked, add the remaining chopped parsley. Pour over the cooked pasta shells. (1 serving amounts to 337/1415 Cal/J)

Note:

This sauce can be prepared using smoked bacon. In this case chop the bacon finely and fry in the oil before adding garlic and parsley.

Noodles with Truffles

(serves 4-6)

400 g. (14 oz. noodles), 80 g. (3 oz.) butter
60 - 80 g. (2 - 3 oz.) truffles, salt
peppercorns, 300 ml. (10 fl. oz.) fresh cream
grated cheese

Cook the noodles in salted water and drain. Clean the truffles well and wash them. Slice finely into small slices or thin strips. Sauté for about 2 minutes in butter over a low heat, after seasoning with a little salt. Pour the cream into the pan and cook briefly. Stir in the grated cheese and pepper. Pour the sauce over the cooked noodles. (1 serving amounts to 472/1982 Cal/J).

Tip:

If you wish to bring out the aroma and taste of the truffles, add a couple of truffle oil drops into the sauce. In this case, add a smaller quantity of fresh truffles.

Green Maneštra

(serves 6-8)

750 g. (1.5 lb.) smoked pork (head, ribs, knuckles)	
300 g. (11 oz.) smoked mutton	
100 g. (4 oz.) smoked bacon	
1 kg. (2 lb.) collard greens	
750 g. (1.75 lb.) fresh cabbage	
2 - 3 cloves garlic	
salt	
pepper	
1 tablespoon Vegeta	

*M*anestra, menestra, or manistria is soup that can be linked with the most famous Italian soup - minestre or minestrone. As its name tells us, anything can be added to this big soup, ranging from smoked bacon, prosciutto (Parma ham), to various vegetables, rice and pasta. Green manestra from Dubrovnik and Župa, made of several sorts of cabbage vegetables, jota and maneštra od bobiči, and maneštra from Istria lack none of the tastiness of the Milanese minestrone. These thick soups, independent dishes in themselves, have their winter and summer tastes, because the contents of the soup-pot depend on the season and the foodstuffs at hand.

Bring the smoked meat briefly to the boil and strain.
Put the meat into fresh water and continue cooking. Briefly boil the collard greens in hot water. Strain and cut into wide strips.
Place the cooked meat on a plate. Cut the potato into cubes and cook in the soup.

When half done, add the collard greens and fresh cabbage cut into strips. Add the bacon and garlic, previously chopped together, and Vegeta. Add water and cook until all the ingredients are tender.

Separate the smoked meat from the bones and cut into small pieces. Stir into the maneštra and season with salt and pepper to taste.

(1 serving amounts to 745/3129 Cal/J)

Pasta and Beans

(serves 4-6)

400 g. (14 oz.) beans
250 g. (9 oz.) short pasta
4 tablespoons oil
100 g. (4 oz.) smoked bacon
1 onion
bay leaf
parsley leaf
celery leaf
1 soup cube
salt
pepper
2 cloves garlic
1 tablespoon tomato puree

Soak the beans and then boil briefly. Strain them and cook again in fresh water. In the meantime, fry the sliced bacon and onion.

Stir into the half-cooked beans. Add the bay leaf, celeriac leaves, soup cube and pasta. Mix well, and add water if necessary, leave to cook slowly until everything is tender. When almost cooked, salt to taste, add the tomato puree, chopped garlic and parsley leaves.

(1 serving amounts to 595/2499 Cal/J)

Tip:

The pasta may be cooked separately, but then it should be added to the beans when they are completely done.

*I*n any continental region, stews and soups are thickened with browned flour, but in the
Primorje region or its hinterland this would be unheard of. Cooks there prefer their
solution for maneštras, sauces and the like, and that is: pešt or pesto. It is prepared by finely
chopping together (almost to a paste-like consistency) smoked bacon, garlic and parsley
leaves. Pešt may also be prepared using a blender. It is added to the soup at the beginning, so
that the bacon can lose its compactness.

Thick Soup with Sweet Corn

(serves 4-6)

50 g. (2 oz.) young corn from the cob
or canned corn, 300 g. (10 oz.) beans
600 g. (1 lb. 5 oz.) potatoes
100 g. (4 oz.) smoked bacon
100 g. (4 oz.) smoked meat or prosciutto
(Parma ham), 3 cloves garlic
parsley and celeriac leaves
50 ml. (2 fl. oz.) olive oil
salt, pepper, 1 tablespoon Vegeta

Soak the beans and then boil them briefly.
Strain, and put in fresh water to cook together with the smoked meat.
Add the "pešt" into the half-cooked beans.
Add the corn as well as the chopped celeriac leaves, cubed potatoes, oil, salt, pepper and Vegeta. Simmer slowly until everything is tender. Take out the meat and cut into slices. Before serving, sprinkle the maneštra with chopped parsley.

(1 serving amounts to 577/2423 Cal/J)

Tip:

Instead of smoked meat you can cook a prosciutto (Parma ham) bone (or bacon or ham bone) in the soup.

Istrian Jota (Stew)

(serves 4-6)

200 g. (7 oz.) beans
500 g. (18 oz.) sauerkraut
300 g. (11 oz.) potatoes
400 (14 oz.) smoked ribs or other cured
meat
80 g. (3 oz.) smoked bacon
3 cloves garlic
salt
peppercorns
2 bay leaves

Soak the beans. Bring briefly to the boil.
Strain them and boil some more in fresh water. Put the washed sauerkraut and smoked ribs to cook in a separate pan.
When the beans are half-cooked, add together with the soup to the sauerkraut. Add the bay leaves, peppercorns, salt and bacon and garlic chopped together (pešt). Then add the cubed potatoes and cook until everything is tender. Take the meat out of the soup, cut into pieces and serve separately with the jota.

(1 serving amounts to 524/2201 Cal/J)

Tip:

You can make the jota thicker by mashing part of the beans and potatoes.

Arambašići
(Stuffed Sauerkraut Rolls)
(serves 6-8)

2 heads of sauerkraut
700 g. (1.5 lb.) minced beef (fatty, neck parts)
300 g. (11 oz.) minced pork
150 g. (5 oz.) smoked bacon
1 onion
2 - 3 garlic cloves
nutmeg
cinnamon powder
2 cloves
pepper
salt
1 egg
1 tablespoon lard
cured mutton or
other cured meat (ribs, neck)

Place the minced meat in a bowl. Dice the bacon finely, fry briefly in a pan, add chopped onion and continue frying until the onion is glassy, and then add to the meat. Add chopped garlic, some grated nutmeg, a little cinnamon powder, crushed cloves, pepper, salt and egg. Mix the ingredients well. If too compact, add a little water.

Take a cabbage head, separate the leaves, carve the thickness off the central stems. If the leaves are big, cut them in half. Put a spoonful of the meat mixture on each leaf and roll up the arambašići, beginning from the stem side. Tuck in the sides well so they will not become loose when cooking. Put the lard into the saucepan, cover with remaining cabbage leaves. Arrange the arambašići on top so they fit snugly.

Place a peace of cured meat between the arambašići. Pour in enough water to cover everything, place a lid on the saucepan and simmer over a low heat for about 3 hours. Do not stir during cooking, but only shake the saucepan occasionally.

(1 serving amounts to 553/2323 Cal/J)

S *arma (cabbage rolls) is a universal*

dish today, popular throughout Croatia. It origi-

nates from the Orient. Most often it is served in winter. But there are less known

variants besides the classical meat stuffing rolled up in a sauerkraut leaf. Sarma may be made with fresh

cabbage, Swiss chard, collard greens, or even vine leaves when only mixed minced meat is used as stuffing,

usually pork and beef, but also lamb and mutton. These sarmas are smaller in size and often seasoned with

aromatic seasonings - nutmeg, cloves, cinnamon - especially known in the Dalmatian hinterland as Sinj or

Benkovac arambašići, harambašići, and in Herzegovina as japrak.

Chicken Primošten Style

(serves 4-6)

1 chicken (about 1.2 kg. /3 lb.)
30 g. (1 oz.) flour
5 tablespoons oil
60 g. (2 oz.) prosciutto (Parma ham) or smoked bacon
150 g. (5 oz.) onion
6 small fresh tomatoes (or 2 tablespoons tomato puree)
3 cloves garlic
1 tablespoon Vegeta
50 ml. (2 fl. oz.) Prosecco (Sherry)
2 tablespoons capers
500 g. (18 oz.) peas
500 g. (18 oz.) new potatoes
salt, pepper
parsley

Wash the chicken and cut into pieces. Sprinkle the chicken with salt and flour, fry in hot oil until brown on all sides. Remove the chicken from the pan. Briefly fry the cubed prosciutto (Parma ham) or bacon with the chopped onion. Add the peeled and diced tomatoes, chopped garlic, and then add the chicken pieces. Sprinkle with Vegeta, pour in the Prosecco diluted with a little water. Add the capers and peas and continue cooking until the meat is tender. Add a little water, if necessary. When the meat is almost cooked, add the cubed potatoes, and the pepper. Finally, add the chopped parsley leaves.

(1 serving amounts to 724/3041 Cal/J)

Chicken used to be served only on festive occasions in the past, while today it is eaten almost daily. The meat is light, and dishes containing it are also light, but this is usually compensated by adding potatoes, pasta or vegetables. What does remain of the traditional cooking is the use of aromatic coastal herbs, such as bay leaves, rosemary, capers ...

Fowl Brodetto

(serves 4-6)

1 medium-sized hen
2 tablespoons grape brandy
40 g. (1.5 oz.) oil
1 onion
100 ml. (4 fl. oz.) white wine
2 cloves garlic
4 fresh tomatoes
parsley
salt
pepper
allspice
bay leaf
rosemary
1 lemon slice
1 tablespoon Vegeta

Cut the hen into pieces, sprinkle with salt, Vegeta and grape brandy. Let the meat rest awhile.

Fry the chopped onion in hot oil, add chopped garlic and parsley, peeled and cubed tomatoes, allspice, pepper, bay leaf, rosemary and slice of lemon. Add the prepared pieces of meat. Add a little warm water and simmer slowly until everything becomes tender. Serve with polenta.

(1 serving amounts to 857/3599 Cal/J)

Needle Macaroni

(serves 8-10)

1 kg (2 lb.) flour
1 egg
1 egg yolk
100 g. (4 oz.) butter
50 ml. (2 fl. oz.) oil, salt
150 - 200 ml. (5 - 8 fl. oz.) lukewarm water

Place the flour on the working surface. Make a well in it for the egg, egg yolk, salt, oil and softened butter. Add lukewarm water gradually to the above ingredients, and mix into a dough. Knead the dough well, so that it is smooth, but neither too soft, nor too firm.

Divide into several pieces, cover with a cloth, and leave to rest. Make small rolls from the dough, cut into small pieces. Put each piece around a knitting needle and make macaroni with the palms of the hands, sliding them off the needle. When you have mastered this, you will be able to make two macaroni at a time.

Make macaroni from all of the dough and arrange on a floured surface to dry for a short time.

Cook the macaroni in boiling, salted water. Strain and then sprinkle with a little oil. Mix gently and serve as side dish with meat. You can serve macaroni as an independent meal sprinkled with melted butter, and grated Pag cheese.

(1 serving amounts to 405/1701 Cal/J)

Istrian "Fuži" (Pasta)

(serves 4)

350 g. (12 oz.) flour
2 eggs, 1 tablespoon oil
2 tablespoons white wine, salt

Sift the flour onto a working surface, make a well in the centre. Put the oil, wine and salt with a little water into this well and knead a firm dough from these ingredients. Roll out the dough into thin sheets. Cut into 3-4 cm (1 inch) wide strips, and then cut the strips into pieces which are 3-4 (1 inch) long.

Make fuži by folding over two opposing corners of each piece, pressing them down firmly with the finger. Arrange them on a floured surface and leave to dry for a short time.

Boil the pasta in salted water. Strain and serve as a side dish.

(1 serving amounts to 386/1621 Cal/J)

Fine Goulash

(serves 4)

600 g. (1.5 lb.) lamb
4 tablespoons oil
40 g. (1.5 oz.) smoked bacon
2 onions
1 tablespoon tomato puree, salt
Vegeta, nutmeg, a clove
pepper, 1 tablespoon flour, parsley
40 g. (1.5 oz.) sheep milk cheese

Cut the meat into pieces, fry briefly in hot oil. When the meat browns, add the chopped bacon and onions. Fry briefly. Sprinkle with salt, Vegeta, and cook for about an hour and a half, adding water when necessary. When almost cooked, add tomato puree, grated nutmeg, the clove, pepper and flour mixed in a little water. Continue cooking for about ten minutes. Before serving, add chopped parsley and grated cheese.

Serve this tasty goulash with needle macaroni, fuži, or some other ready-made pasta.

(1 serving amounts to 565/2373 Cal/J)

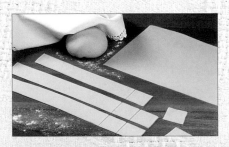

*A*lthough any goulash story usually begins in Hungary or the Pannonian steppes, Croatians are also proud of their recipes for extensive preparations and long cooking of beef or veal together with onions, whether this applies to the northern flatlands or the southern mountains. Žgvacet made from veal, turkey, chicken, rabbit, or wild game is characteristic to Istria and the Northern Adriatic Islands. The side dish is usually polenta or fine, soft pasta which needs considerable effort, if home-made. Istrian fuži and posutice or needle macaroni are still prepared and served today, but mainly on festive occasions, such as weddings. Those who love goulash even say that the secret of the taste is actually in the pasta.

129

In Dalmatia each piece of good meat is usually made into a pašticada - a cult dish in Dalmatia. The meat is larded with bacon and garlic and then basted with good vinegar during cooking.

In the continental parts pasta with potatoes, various dumplings and similar dishes are popular. The Dalmatians are very keen on gnocchi (potato dumplings). Pašticada is not complete without gnocchi. But this carefully formed dough, the size of a walnut, is often combined with other sauces made from meat, cheese, cream, mushrooms and vegetables.

Gnocchi

(serves 8-10)

500 g. (18 oz.) white potatoes
150 - 200 g. (5-7 oz.) flour
1 egg, 1 egg yolk
60 g. (2 oz.) butter or lard
salt

Boil the potatoes, peel, and mash while still hot. Add flour, butter or lard, egg and egg yolk, salt to taste and make a dough. Divide it into 2 - 3 pieces, form each piece into a roll. Slice the rolls into equal pieces. Arrange the pieces on a floured working surface and leave to rest short time.
Press each piece over a fine grater with the thumb so that the gnocchi are more decorative-looking.
Put the gnocchi in a large quantity of salted water and boil. After the gnocchi have risen to the surface, boil for one more minute. Take them out of the water and strain.
(1 serving amounts to 154/647 Cal/J).

Beef with Gnocchi
(serves 8-10)

2 kg. (4.5 lb.) beef or round of veal
200 g. (7 oz.) smoked bacon, 200 g. (7 oz.) onions
150 g. (5 oz.) parsley root, 150 g. (5 oz.) carrots
50 g. (2 oz.) celeriac root, 2 cloves garlic
20 g. /2/3 oz.) tomato puree
150 - 200 ml. (5 - 8 fl. oz.) oil
1 - 2 tablespoons Vegeta, 6 prunes
300 (10 fl. oz.) red wine
2 tablespoons mustard, bay leaf
rosemary, thyme, salt pepper

Wash the meat, dry it, and lard with bacon strips. Rub salt into the meat, and spread the mustard and oil over the surface. Leave to rest at least 2 hours or overnight. Briefly brown the meat on all sides in hot oil. Remove it from the pan, and briefly fry the sliced onions and garlic, and other vegetables cut into strips in the same pan. Return the meat to the pan, sprinkle with Vegeta, cover and stew for about two hours, adding small quantities of water and wine mixture from time to time, to keep the meat moist. When the meat is half cooked, add diluted tomato puree, and then the washed prunes. When cooking is almost completed, add the bay leaf, rosemary, thyme, pepper to taste, and salt, if necessary. Take the meat out of the saucepan, cut into slices and arrange on a heated plate. Puree the vegetables with the sauce, cook briefly and pour over the meat. Potato gnocchi go best with beef prepared in this way. (1 serving amounts to 761/3196 Cal/J)

Lamb
à la pašticada
(serves 6-8)

1 leg of lamb (about 2 kg/4.5 lb.)
50 g. (2 oz.) prosciutto (Parma ham)
garlic, peppercorns, salt
100 ml. (4 fl. oz.) oil, 200 g. (7 oz.) onions
200 g. (7 oz.) carrots
1 tablespoon tomato puree
200 ml. (8 fl. oz.) red wine
50 ml. (2 fl. oz.) prosecco
2 tablespoons wine vinegar
celeriac and parsley leaves
bay leaf, rosemary, clove
1 teaspoon flour, 1 tablespoon Vegeta

Bone the meat and spread out into a large steak.

Beat with a kitchen mallet, sprinkle with chopped garlic, season with salt and pepper. Arrange small prosciutto (Parma ham) pieces over the meat.

Roll up the meat, tie with thread and season with salt. Fry briefly on all sides in hot oil in a big pan, remove and set aside.

Fry chopped onions and sliced carrots in the same pan.

Add tomato puree, Vegeta, pour in the red wine, prosecco and wine vinegar. Then add the celeriac leaves, peppercorns, bay leaf, rosemary and the clove. Return the meat to the pan and stew for about 1 hour, adding water occasionally.

When the meat is tender, remove it, and puree the vegetables. Add flour mixed with water to the sauce, and cook briefly. You can make the sauce thinner by adding water or stock.

Remove the thread and carve the meat into slices. Arrange on a warmed plate, pour hot sauce over the meat slices and sprinkle with chopped parsley.

Serve with gnocchi or wide noodles as a side dish.

(1 serving amounts to 645/2709 Cal/J)

*T*radition is strong enough to withstand the internationalisation of the national cuisine. With developing tourism, cooks have been inspired to create new, healthier and more economical dishes. Lamb à la pašticada is one if these dishes, created in the Split hotel Bellevue, to suit the taste of contemporary gourmets.

Wild Rabbit Goulash

(serves 4)

1 rabbit (about 1.2 kg / 2 lb. 7 oz.)
100 ml. (4 fl. oz.) oil
100 g. onion
3 cloves garlic
salt, pepper
100 - 200 ml. (4 - 8 fl. oz.) white wine
thyme
rosemary
bay leaf
15 g. 1/2 oz.) flour
1 tablespoon tomato puree

Prepare the marinade mixture according to the recipe below for Roast Rabbit in Sauce, excluding the cloves from the ingredients. When the marinade cools, pour it over the skinned and washed rabbit. Marinate for twenty-four hours.

Take the rabbit out of the marinade, dry it, cut into smaller pieces. Brown the pieces on all sides in hot oil. Add finely chopped onions and garlic, stew briefly. Add the pepper, thyme, rosemary and bay leaf. Cover and continue stewing over a low heat. As necessary, add the remaining wine and marinade. When the meat becomes tender, add the tomato puree and the flour mixed in a little water. Cook briefly.

Serve this goulash with fuži, gnocchi, macaroni or polenta.

(1 serving amounts to 679/2852 Cal/J)

Roast Rabbit in Sauce

(serves 4-6)

1 rabbit
100 g. (4 oz.) lard
100 g. (4 oz.) smoked bacon
1 lemon
40. g. (1.5 oz.) flour
20 g. (2/3 oz.) sugar
Marinade:
250 ml. (12 fl. oz.) wine vinegar
100 g. (4 oz.) carrots
50 g. (2 oz.) celeriac
80 g. (3 oz.) parsley root
several peppercorns and whortleberries (huckleberries)
10 cloves, 5 bay leaves
salt, Vegeta, water

Marinade:

Put the vinegar, finely sliced carrots, celeriac root and parsley root, peppercorns, huckleberries, cloves, bay leaves, salt and Vegeta into water and boil for about 1 hour. Cool the marinade.

Cut the skinned and washed rabbit into large pieces, arrange them in a bowl and pour the cool marinade over them. Marinate for about 24 hours. Take the meat out of the marinade, lard it with bacon strips. Place the rabbit pieces into a roasting pan with a small amount of lard in it, cover well with aluminium foil, and place in a hot oven. As necessary, add water to the pan. When almost completely done, remove the foil and continue roasting.

While the meat is roasting in the oven, prepare the sauce. Fry the sugar in hot lard, mixing constantly, until it browns. Then add the vegetables with spices from the marinade and the lemon rind. Stew, adding marinade liquid when necessary. Remove the vegetables when tender and puree them, mixing in the flour diluted in a little water. Add some juices from the roast and cook briefly.

Arrange the roasted rabbit meat in the prepared sauce. Serve with potato gnocchi as a side dish.

(1 serving amounts to 649/2726 Cal/J)

Wild game has always been in demand and in the past was considered as a delicacy, for discerning palates only. This is why there are special cookbooks containing only wild game recipes. Nowadays eating game meat is considered by some to be an atavistic regression, while others regard game meat as a delicacy, and even as an aphrodisiac. It is said that hunters are the best wild game cooks. Just as hunting is increasingly becoming a sport and leisure time preoccupation, so wild game dishes, too, are changing. Classical recipes are coming back and new interesting ones are being created. Wild hare is sometimes substituted by domestic rabbit.

The custom in Croatia to exhibit lambs roasting on the spit at road-side taverns is no older than a couple of decades. It expanded with the development of tourism because tourists were impressed by this manner of cooking meat, close to Nature. Lamb, and suckling pig meat roasted over a spit fire is usually served with spring onions, tomatoes and peppers. The method of baking lamb and even kid meat under a peka or čripnja, considered to give tastier meat, is not so well known. This is characteristic to the entire Mediterranean coastal region and its hinterland. In Sinj, this tradition has remained the same since the time of the Illyrians and has not changed for at least 3000 years. Today's roasts taken from the oven rely on special herbs to produce their tempting aromas.

Roast Lamb

(serves 6)

lamb leg (about 2.5 kg. /5.5 lb.)
100 ml. (4 fl. oz.)
bay leaf
rosemary, salt
Vegeta
1 onion
1 head of garlic

Wash the meat and rub it with a mixture of salt and Vegeta. Put the meat into a baking dish and pour hot oil over it. Put around

the meat a rosemary sprig, bay leaf, onion and an unpeeled head of garlic cut into quarters.

Add 100 ml. (4 fl. oz.) of hot water and cover well with foil. Roast in a well heated oven for about 90 minutes at 220° C/425° F/Gas Mark 7. When nearly done, remove the foil so that the meat can turn golden brown. Baste with the roasting juices, as necessary. Cut the roast meat into pieces. Strain the roasting juices and serve separately. Serve with baked potatoes, spring onions, tomatoes or salad per choice.

You can bake the potatoes together with the meat. In this case, place the potatoes in the baking dish when the meat is half done.

(1 serving amounts to 873/3667 Cal/J)

rutti di mare, or fruits of the sea, are a true delight for any gourmet. They are prepared so as to taste as if just taken out of the sea. As soon as they learn to walk, children who grow up beside the Adriatic learn how to find limpets and how to suck out their goodness. Connoisseurs delight in fresh oysters sprinkled with a few drops of lemon juice. Croatia's best oysters come from Malostonski Canal in the south and Limski Canal and the bays around Pula in the north. Gourmets serve other shellfish and crayfish, even the "queen of the Adriatic" - the sea-spider which can be found only along the western coast of the Istrian peninsula in the most simple manner, baked and garnished with the simplest biblical dressing and seasonings - olive oil, wine vinegar, pepper, garlic, parsley ...

Sea-Spider Salad

(serves 4)

4 sea-spiders, 100 ml. (4 fl. oz.) olive oil
wine vinegar, 4 garlic cloves
salt, white pepper, parsley

Wash the sea-spiders and boil in water for about 30 minutes, immersing the backs first. When they have cooled down, separate the claws and legs from the bodies, crack the shells with a pounder and take out the flesh. Wash the shells well inside and out, taking care not to damage them.

Place the flesh in a bowl, cut the bigger pieces into slices, season with finely chopped garlic and parsley. Add salt, oil and vinegar to taste and pepper generously. Mix gently, cover and refrigerate.
First place a lettuce leaf into each of the prepared shells, and spoon in the sea-spider salad. Arrange on a platter and garnish with lettuce strips, lemon slices and olives.

(1 serving amounts to 274/1151 Cal/J)

Oysters with Lemon

(serves 1)

6 oysters, 1 lemon
30 g. (1 oz.) butter, toast

Open the fresh oysters with a special knife and separate carefully from the shell. Place the meat and the juice into the deeper shell. Arrange on a platter covered with crushed ice. Serve with lemon slices, butter and toast.

(1 serving amounts to 578/2428 Cal/J)

Salads made from molluscs - octopus, cuttle-fish, squid, musk octopus - are usual hors d'oeuvres in fish restaurants everywhere, not only by the seaside. These salads and cod à la white, special dishes prepared in Croatia during fasting at Christmas and Easter, would not taste the same if they were not prepared with olive oil. This applies to many other Dalmatian dishes. Today's recipes contain this ingredient in smaller quantities, and the oil is lighter, refined from the oil produced in small oil-producing units and stored in old stone vessels. For thousands of years olive-groves have been a source of authentic wealth. Production and trade in preserved green and black olives meant real prosperity for those living on the Adriatic coast. The oil from Krk was so famous that it is always present when ancient Roman writers described patrician feasts and amphorae from sunken vessels. Happily, olive growing is being revived.

Octopus Salad

(serves 4)

1 small octopus (about 1 kg./2 lb.)
50 ml. (2 fl. oz.) wine vinegar
100 ml. (4 fl. oz.) olive oil
2 cloves garlic
2 small onions
salt
pepper
Vegeta

Wash the octopus. Be sure that the suckers are cleaned of sand. Place the octopus in a saucepan of cold water and cook until tender. Drain saving a little of the stock. Cut into pieces. Salt to taste, add chopped onion and pour oil over the octopus pieces. Put the boiling water, vinegar and a pinch of Vegeta in a separate pan. Boil briefly, add chopped garlic and pepper. Pour this marinade over the octopus pieces, mix well and set aside to cool.

(1 serving amounts to 420/1764 Cal/J)

Squid and Cuttle-Fish Salad

(serves 4)

400 g. (14 oz.) squid
400 g. (14 oz.) cuttle-fish
100 ml. (4 fl. oz.) olive oil
50 ml. (2 fl. oz.) vinegar
3 cloves garlic
salt
pepper
parsley

Cook the cleaned and washed squid and cuttle-fish in plenty of water. When they are tender, drain them - save part of the soup - and leave to cool. Slice into small pieces. Now salt them because the flesh toughens if cooked in salted water. Pour oil and vinegar over them, add a little soup. Pepper to taste, sprinkle with chopped parsley and mix well.

Always chill frutti di mare salads well before serving.

(1 serving amounts to 405/1701 Cal/J)

Cod à la white

(serves 6)

400 g. (14 oz.) dried cod
200 ml. (8 fl. oz.) olive oil, 5 - 6 cloves garlic parsley, salt and pepper

Pound the cod with a wooden pounder and then soak in cold water at least 2 days. Work the cod frequently with the hands, and change the water daily.

Place the softened cod in a saucepan of cold water. Add salt as soon as the water comes to the boil. Remove it from the heat and leave aside for 10 minutes. Drain the cod and save the water. Place the cod pieces on a clean cloth. Clean the fish pieces of skin and bone. Place the cleaned and flaked cod in a bowl, pepper to taste and pour oil over it. Sprinkle with chopped garlic and parsley. Cover the bowl. Shake it up and down vigorously until the cod turns white. Place the bowl in a saucepan of boiling water and cook over steam for about 1 hour over a gentle heat.

Serve hot or as chilled hors-d'oeuvres with toast.

Tip:

You can shorten preparation time by cooking the cod completely and then mixing it with the other ingredients in a mixer.
In this case, more olive oil is needed.

(1 serving amounts to 425/1785 Cal/J)

S tone soup is no anecdote! Those in the know make a tasty soup even from algae-covered stones, in the pores of which there are small shellfish and crayfish. This may seem to indicate famine or extreme poverty, but real gourmets regard this soup as the peak of culinary art. The same applies to excellent soups cooked from various fish. After cooking fish such as cod, dentex, grey mullet, red scorpionfish or some other white fish - the more types the better - the stock always remains. One can boil rice in it, or put in small fish pieces or the vegetables that were cooked in the stock. A thick soup containing all the pureed ingredients would be even richer.

It is interesting to note that pasta was never added to soups in Dalmatia. Rice is prepared by placing the washed grains into hot oil and frying them until glassy, stirring constantly. The fried rice is seasoned with salt and then the fish soup is poured over it. The soup is left to simmer until the rice is tender. Rice can also be cooked separately and added to the soup before serving.

Fish Bouillon

(serves 4-6)

1 kg. (2 lb.) white sea fish
1 onion
4 garlic cloves
1 carrot
1 parsley root
celeriac
Vegeta
lemon
bay leaf
salt
peppercorns
50 ml. (2 fl. oz.) olive oil
parsley

Place the diced carrot, parsley root, onion, garlic cloves and celeriac in a large pot and cover with water. Add a little Vegeta, salt, several peppercorns, bay leaf and 1 - 2 lemon slices. Boil briefly, and then add the cleaned fish, whole. Continue simmering over a very low heat for about 10 - 15 minutes, depending on the size of the fish. Carefully remove the cooked fish from the soup, and serve separately. Drain the soup. Add a little more ground pepper to the soup, then add the lemon juice and olive oil. Serve the soup with boiled rice and chopped parsley.

(1 serving amounts to 115/483 Cal/J)

Thick Fish Soup

(serves 4-6)

500 g. (1 lb.) white sea fish
lemon, 50 ml. (2 fl. oz.) olive oil
1 small onion, 1 carrot
1 parsley root
2 cloves garlic, 1 potato
salt, pepper cloves
1 tablespoon tomato puree
100 ml. (4 fl. oz.) white wine, bay leaf
celeriac leaf

Place the fish, thinly sliced carrot, parsley and onion, and peeled and sliced potato in cold water and heat. Add the bay leaf, pepper cloves, salt, celery leaf and a little olive oil. Cook the fish slowly for about 15 minutes. Take the fish out of the soup, clean it of bones and cut into small pieces. Strain the soup, puree the vegetables and return to the soup together with the fish. Add tomato puree, wine, chopped garlic and the remaining oil. Bring briefly to the boil. When the soup is cooked, sprinkle with parsley, more pepper to taste and lemon juice.

(1 serving amounts to 229/962 Cal/J)

Perhaps it is hard to believe that rice did not arrive from the Far and Near East - not even in Italy, the homeland of risotto - before the 15th century. Since then this cheap, practically imperishable and always reliable standby has become an important item in international trade, as well as part of simple, but also refined Dalmatian dishes. It is interesting how popular this plant, which grows in water and can not even be cooked without water, has become a staple in the part of country where barren rocks dominate. A risotto will be tastier if soup is added from time to time while the risotto is cooking, and if frutti di mare are included as well. Black risotto is a dish which incorporates the black liquid which squids use to defend themselves from predators.

Sailor's Risotto

(serves 4-6)

300 g. (11 oz.) rice
200 g. (7 oz.) squid, 200 g. (7 oz.) shellfish
200 g. (7 oz.) small scampi
100 ml. (4 fl. oz.) olive oil
40 g. (1.5 oz.) butter
1 small onion
3 cloves garlic, 200 g. (7 oz.) tomatoes
150 ml. (5 fl. oz.) dry white wine
salt, pepper, parsley

Fry the finely chopped onion in a mixture of olive oil and butter. Add the chopped parsley, sliced squid, and followed immediately by the cleaned shellfish and scampi. Fry briefly, add the peeled and diced tomatoes.

Boil the rice in a separate pan in lightly salted water. When the rice is half-cooked, strain it and mix with the squid, shellfish and scampi. Add wine to the risotto and sauté, stirring constantly, adding water occasionally. Salt and pepper to taste and mix in the chopped parsley.

Serve with grated cheese, according to taste.

(1 serving amounts to 519/2180 Cal/J)

Tip:

Good risotto should not be dry, but moist, so it should be stirred slowly, with the addition of liquid from time to time. At the same time care should be taken not to overcook the rice.

Note:

You can prepare spaghetti with frutti di mare in a similar manner. In this case mix some wine into the sauce, and then the cooked spaghetti.

Risotto with Scampi

(serves 4-6)

*300 g. (11 oz.) rice, 300 g. (11 oz.) cleaned
scampi tails, 100 ml. (4 fl. oz.) olive oil and
sunflower oil mixture, 40 g. (1.5 oz.) butter
3 cloves garlic, salt, freshly ground pepper
30 ml. (1 fl. oz.) brandy
150 g. (5 fl. oz.) white wine, 200 ml. (8 fl. oz.)
fresh cream, parsley, Vegeta*

Boil the rice in salted boiling water. Drain when
it is half-cooked. Save part of the cooking liquid. Gently heat the oil in a wide pan. Briefly
fry the chopped garlic. Add the washed and
dried scampi tails. Salt and fry. After brief sautéing, add cognac. Set alight the cognac, and
put out the flame with wine. Boil briefly. Mix in
the prepared rice, Vegeta and cook, stirring and
occasionally adding the liquid left over after
boiling the rice. When almost cooked, add
fresh cream, butter and chopped parsley. Pepper to taste and stir the risotto well.
(1 serving amounts to 597/2507 Cal/J)

Black Risotto

(serves 4-6)

*150 ml. (5 fl. oz.) olive oil, 200 g. 7 oz.) onion
300 g. (11 oz.) small cuttle-fish
200 g. (7 oz.) squid, 2 sachets squid ink
250 g. (9 oz.) scampi, 400 g. (14 oz.) shellfish
bay leaf, lemon juice and rind, parsley
3 cloves garlic, salt, pepper
250 ml. (12 fl. oz.) white wine
300 g. (11 oz.) rice, Vegeta*

Clean the squid and cut into thin slices.
Wash the cuttle-fish and chop finely.
Fry finely chopped onions in 100 ml. (4 fl.
oz.) oil. Add the prepared squid and cuttle-
fish and sauté for about 10 minutes. Pour
half of the water and wine mixture over the
ingredients. Add Vegeta, bay leaf, lemon
juice and 1 lemon slice. Cook for about 30
minutes. In the meantime add the squid
black ink.
Fry the scampi in the remaining oil. Cover

and sauté for about 5 minutes. Add chopped
parsley, garlic and shellfish. When the shellfish open, pour the remaining wine over
this, the prepared cuttle-fish and squid, and
the half-cooked rice. Fold in gently and cook
slowly (mind that the rice does not overcook).
A little butter can be stirred into the risotto
when it is cooked. Serve immediately on a
hot plate.
(1 serving amounts to 657/2759 Cal/J)

Note:
When preparing black risotto you must take
care to use the black ink of fresh squid or
cuttle-fish only. Frozen ink is neither tasty
nor effective.

Tip:
In order to keep the black ink fresh, leave it
in its own sack in a glass with a little oil.
Keep refrigerated.

The largest Adriatic cephalopod - octopus or musk octopus - can grow up to 1.3 m in length and weigh as much as 15 kg. Octopus vulgaris is better known for legends about its size and the invincible strength of its eight suckered arms, than for its flesh. In spite of this it was caught by inhabitants living inland on Velebit mountain or in the hills surrounding Dubrovnik, far away from the sea. The people living on the islands knew how to prepare many delicacies. Octopus was dried in the sun on the island of Rab and in the town of Rab, and prepared with eggs over an open fire on days when fishermen did not go out to sea. It was boiled on the island of Pag. The inhabitants of Hvar and Lastovo roasted it under pekas, in wine, and on the island of Vis in an ancient manner, on hot rocks by the sea. Various molluscs were prepared in a similar manner.

Octopus Novalja Style

(serves 4-6)

1 kg. (2 lb.) octopus
1.5 kg. (3.5 lb.) potatoes, 4 - 5 cloves garlic
150 ml. (5 fl. oz.) olive oil, or a mixture of olive and sunflower oil, parsley
freshly ground pepper, salt, Vegeta

Place the cleaned octopus to cook in warm water; the water must be unsalted or the meat becomes tough. When the octopus is almost tender, add peeled potatoes cut in halves and a little Vegeta. Boil for about 30 minutes more. Strain the octopus and save the cooking water. Cut the octopus into small pieces and place them on a plate. Add the potatoes, mash them partly with a fork, adding the oil and a part of the cooking water. Then add chopped garlic and parsley, and pepper to taste. Mix well, adding salt if necessary. Serve warm as a separate meal, or as hot hors d'oeuvres.
(1 serving amounts to 605/2541 Cal/J)

Octopus Hvar Style

(serves 4)

1 octopus (about 1 kg./2 lb.)
1 kg. (2 lb.) potatoes
1 large onion
3 cloves garlic
6 tablespoons olive oil
6 tablespoons sunflower oil
salt, pepper
rosemary
100 ml. (4 fl. oz.) white wine
parsley, 1 tablespoon Vegeta

Clean the octopus, place in a baking pan on cold oil. Arrange the peeled potatoes cut into halves on both sides and peeled onion cut into four. Sprinkle with rosemary and Vegeta. Sprinkle a little salt over the potatoes. Cover tightly with aluminium foil and bake without adding water in a preheated oven for about one hour at 180°C/350°F/ Gas Mark 4. When almost done, pour wine over all of the ingredients, add chopped garlic and bake a little while longer, uncovered.

Cut the octopus into pieces and arrange on a preheated plate together with the potatoes, and roasting juices. Sprinkle with chopped parsley.

(1 serving amounts to 737/3095 Cal/J)

Tip:

The foil covering the pan must stick firmly to the pan sides, so that the ingredients stay juicy.

Note:

If you have an octopus that has just been caught and taken out of the sea, it is better first to clean it and freeze it. It will cook more quickly and be more tender.

Fried Squid

(serves 4)

1 kg. (2 lb.) squid	
100 g. (4 oz.) flour	
oil for frying	
salt	
lemon	

Clean the squid, wash and drain them well, leave to dry. Slice them into rounds, cover with flour and fry in deep and well heated oil. Place the fried squid on kitchen tissue to absorb the oil. Sprinkle with salt and serve with fried potatoes, lemon or with sauce.

(1 serving amounts to 350/1470 Cal/J)

Stewed Squid

(serves 4)

800 g. (1.5 lb.) squid	
4 tablespoons olive oil (or a mixture of olive and sunflower oil)	
3 - 4 cloves garlic	
parsley	
salt	
pepper	
Vegeta	

Clean the squid, wash and drain them. Arrange the squid side by side in a broad pan. Salt lightly and sprinkle with pepper, chopped garlic, parsley and Vegeta. Cover the saucepan and stew over a low heat until the squid become tender. Do not stir the squid while they are cooking, but shake the pan from time to time.

Serve the prepared squid with boiled Swiss chard, boiled potatoes or salad.

(1 serving amounts to 294/1235 Cal/J)

Note:

Do not stew the squid too long, or they will change colour and become tough.

*T*hanks to freezers, squid are readily available nowadays. As they are very

tasty and may be prepared in many ways, they have become a great

favourite in Croatian cuisine.

The most popular squid dish is fried squid served with the following sauce. Mix

150 ml. (5 fl. oz.) sour cream with 100 g. (4 oz.) mayonnaise. Add finely chopped

capers, pickled cucumber, a small onion, parsley. Salt and pepper to taste and mix

well.

Fried Squid with Potatoes

(serves 4-6)

500 g. (18 oz.) squid
1.5 kg (3.5 lb.) potatoes
100 ml. (4 fl. oz.) olive oil
2 cloves garlic
1 tablespoon Vegeta
parsley
salt and pepper

Clean, wash and slice the squid into 2 cm-wide (3/4 inch) strips. Peel the potatoes and slice them thinly.

Pour half the oil into a heat-resistant casserole dish. Arrange a layer of half the potatoes and sprinkle with salt, then cover with all the squid strips. Sprinkle with pepper, Vegeta, chopped garlic and parsley. Top off with the remaining potatoes, sprinkle with a little salt and pour oil over them. Cover and place in a preheated oven. Bake for about 45 minutes at 220°C/425°F/Gas Mark 7.

(1 serving amounts to 678/2848 Cal/J)

Tip:

Cook the squid in a covered casserole, so that they become tender and remain juicy without basting.

Stuffed Squid

(serves 4-6)

500 g. (18 oz.) squid
4 cloves garlic, parsley, salt pepper
2 tablespoons breadcrumbs
100 ml. (4 fl. oz.) olive oil
1 tablespoon Vegeta

Clean and wash the squid. Cut off the tentacles, chop them finely. Mix them with chopped garlic and parsley, bread crumbs, salt, pepper and Vegeta. Stuff the squid with this mixture, but only half-fill them. Close each one with a tooth pick. Arrange the stuffed squid side by side in a wide casserole dish. Pour the olive oil over them. Cover the casserole dish and braise them for about 20 minutes. Turn the squid during braising.

Serve with potato salad, boiled Swiss chard or other salads, as desired.

(1 serving amounts to 338/1386 Cal/J)

Squid with Prosciutto (Parma ham)

(serves 4-6)

500 g. (18 oz.) squid, 100 ml. (4 fl. oz.) olive
oil, 30 g. (1 oz.) prosciutto (Parma ham)
1 tablespoon breadcrumbs, salt, pepper
100 ml. (4 fl. oz.) white wine

Clean, wash and dry the squid. Slice the prosciutto (Parma ham) very thinly, and cut each
slice into small pieces. Stuff each squid with
prosciutto. Place the stuffed squid to fry in
well heated olive oil, together with the tentacles. Fry briefly on both sides. Sprinkle with
breadcrumbs, pepper, salt, and pour the wine
over them. Arrange the cooked squid and tentacles on a plate, pour the pan juices over
them. Serve with boiled or fried rice.
(1 serving amounts to 269/1130 Cal/J)

Note:
Squid with prosciutto (Parma ham) will be
tasty if grilled. The prosciutto gives them a
very special taste. Take care not to oversalt
them. Salt them after they are done and serve
with salads of the season.

*In the past, if the catch was small, potatoes or polenta were
served with squid so that all the family members could
have a wholesome meal. There is a variety of stuffing for squid
typical for the whole Mediterranean coast. The most simple and
common one is breadcrumbs and garlic. The most sophisticated
stuffings are those containing prosciutto (Parma ham) or chicory.
There is no really good stuffing without olive oil and finely
chopped tentacles, and sometimes a squid or two, as required.*

Shellfish Buzara

(serves 4-6)

2 kg. (4.5 lb.) shellfish (mussels, etc.)

150 ml. (5 fl. oz.) olive oil

4 - 6 cloves garlic, 2 tablespoons breadcrumbs, pepper, 200 ml. (8 fl. oz.) white
wine, parsley, Vegeta

*S*imple buzara is made all along the Adriatic coast. This a dish made without any onion, but with olive oil, garlic, parsley, bread crumbs and wine, and sometimes tomatoes, depending on whether we wish the buzara to be white or red. Our linguists could not find proof about the name of this dish being specific to our coastline on the basis of the Croatian or other neighbouring languages, apart from traces in the Venetian dialect. In Venice today we can still find dishes reminding us of buzara. Just as a reminder: unless you buy them in a jar, mussels are sold raw and alive. Never use a mussel with a cracked shell, or one that is open and will not close as you tap it. That means that it is already dead and should be discarded.

Clean the shellfish well, scraping the shells and washing them in plenty of fresh water. When they open - discard any that do not - add chopped garlic and sprinkle with bread-crumbs. Stir again, pour wine over them, sprinkle with pepper and Vegeta. Simmer for another ten minutes. When cooked, sprinkle with chopped parsley. Place the

shellfish on a plate and pour the sauce over them. Serve this tasty buzara with toasted bread, rubbed with garlic, if desired.
(1 serving amounts to 523/2197 Cal/J)

Tip:
The shellfish will open at the same time if you place them in hot oil in a broad pan over a high flame, and then stir from time to time, or shake the pan.

Note:
If you have large shellfish and wish to serve them in a special way, discard the empty shells, and arrange the full ones on a plate one next to the other. Pour sauce over them.

Scampi Buzara

(serves 4-6)

1.5 kg. fresh scampi
100 ml. (4 fl. oz.) olive oil
200 g. (7 oz.) tomatoes
6 garlic cloves
small bunch parsley
20 g. (2/3 oz.) breadcrumbs
250 ml. (12 fl. oz.) white wine
salt
freshly ground pepper
parsley
Vegeta

Heat the oil. Fry the washed and dried scampi briefly. Add finely chopped garlic and parsley and the peeled and diced tomatoes. Sprinkle with a little Vegeta, salt and pepper. Briefly simmer. Add the washed scampi, sprinkle with breadcrumbs and pour the wine into the pan. Stir and cook for about 10 · 15 minutes covered, over a moderate heat.
(1 serving amounts to 685/2877 Cal/J)

Grilled Scampi

(serves 4-6)

1.6 kg. (3.5 lb.) large scampi
100 ml. (4 fl. oz.) olive oil
salt, 1 lemon, parsley

*A*long with lobster, scampi are the most well-known crustaceans found in the European seas, and those from the Adriatic are the most highly favoured, especially if caught in the waters of the north Adriatic Sea, from Zadar to the Novigradsko Sea, up to Rijeka and the Kamenjak peninsula in Istria, around the Blitvenica lighthouse near Žirje island Žirje, and around the town of Senj. It is said that scampi are the tastiest crustaceans. Whether there are 33 scampi in a kilogram, or when the individual scampi is at its top weight of 300 g. (11 oz.), the rosy, almost transparent flesh is tender and soft. Depending on size, scampi can be fried, baked, rolled in flour, eggs and breadcrumbs and then fried, boiled, mixed into a risotto or made into a very fine dish - with the scampi tails first wrapped in prosciutto (Parma ham) and then threaded onto skewers and grilled.

Wash the scampi, drain and dry with kitchen tissue. Cut the scampi shells on their lower sides with a knife or scissors. Sprinkle with salt, smear with oil and place on a heated grill. Grill them for about 10 minutes at medium temperature - depending on the size of the scampi - turning from time to time. Arrange the grilled scampi on a large heated plate, garnish with sliced lemon and parsley leaves.

(1 serving amounts to 457/1919 Cal/J)

Scampi Kebabs

(serves 4-6)

500 g. (18 oz.) cleaned scampi tails
50 g. (2 oz.) prosciutto (Parma ham)
50 ml. (2 fl. oz.) olive oil, pepper, 1 lemon
200 g. (7 oz.) rice, 20 g. (2/3 oz.) butter parsley, 40 g. (1.5 oz.) grated sheep milk cheese

Wrap a thin prosciutto (Parma ham) slice around each scampi piece. Thread several onto a skewer or kebab stick. Grill, brushing with olive oil from time to time. Cook the rice separately. Mix with a little butter and chopped parsley. Arrange on a heated plate, and place the kebabs on it. Garnish with lemon slices and serve with grated sheep milk cheese.

(1 serving amounts to 396/1663 Cal/J)

Scampi à la parisienne

(serves 4-6)

500 g. (18 oz.) cleaned scampi tails
2 eggs
salt, parsley
1 lemon
flour
frying oil
Sauce:
100 ml. (4 fl. oz.) mayonnaise
200 ml. (8 fl. oz.) sour cream
parsley, salt, pepper
1 tea spoon capers
1 - 2 pickled cucumbers

Dry the scampi tails well, roll in flour and then coat in the mixed eggs. Deep fry for 3-4 minutes in oil. Be careful that the oil does not overheat. Drain well on absorbent paper.
Serve the scampi with boiled rice and cold sauce. Make the sauce by mixing mayonnaise with sour cream. Then season with salt and pepper. Add chopped parsley, capers and cucumbers.

(1 serving amounts to 400/1680 Cal/J)

O ysters, mussels, date-shells, cockles, dog-cockles, finger-fish, Noah's arks, pen shells are only some of the shellfish found in the Adriatic Sea.

Their beauty inspired founding of the famous Shell Museum in Makarska, and the designer, Branka Donassy, who created a very impressive gown which won an award at the Miss World 1996 competition.

But, regrettably, shellfish have not been used in cuisine as much as they could have been. The exception are mussels, particularly in recent years when they have been cultivated. Gourmets like scallops, fan-like, big shell-fish named after the Spanish pilgrims who decorated their clothes with such shells during pilgrimages. They are very tasty boiled, baked and even raw. The best known locations for them in Croatia are the surroundings of Zadar, especially the Novigradsko Sea, Podgorski channel and the western coast of Istria.

Scampi Home Style

(serves 4-6)

1.6 kg. (3.5 lb.) scampi in their shell
100 ml. (4 fl. oz.) olive oil
salt, pepper, Vegeta
4 cloves garlic, parsley

Heat a little oil in a wide pan, fry the cleaned scampi briefly, turn once. Add cold water so the scampi are covered. Sprinkle with 1 tablespoon Vegeta, a little salt, pepper, finely chopped garlic and parsley. Leave to simmer briefly. When cooked, pour cold olive oil over the ingredients.

Arrange the scampi on plates and pour over them the soup in which they were cooked.

(1 serving amounts to 415/1743 Cal/J)

Baked Scallops

(serves 1)

2 - 3 scallops
3 tablespoons finely ground breadcrumbs
parsley, 2 cloves garlic
50 ml. (2 fl. oz.) olive oil
salt, pepper, lemon
20 g. (2/3 oz.) butter

Wash the scallops well, place in a wide pan over a high heat so that they open. Stir occasionally...

Remove the meat from the shells. Place in the deeper half of the shell.

Mix the bread crumbs, chopped parsley, garlic, salt and pepper separately. Add enough oil to obtain a thick mixture and blend well. Mix in a little grated Parmesan cheese, per taste.

Spread the mixture over the shell meat. Top with a little butter and place in a well heated oven to bake for only a few minutes.

Place the baked scallops on a plate, garnish with lemon slices, parsley and serve hot.

(1 serving amounts to 669/2810 Cal/J)

Lobster Cocktail

(serves 4)

250 g. (9 oz.) cooked lobster meat
100 g. (4 oz.) mayonnaise
100 ml. (4 fl. oz.) cream
3 tablespoons tomato ketchup
Worcester sauce
1 tablespoon brandy
Tabasco sauce
lemon juice
salad leaves, salt

Place the salad leaves in goblets. Arrange some lobster meat in each glass. Pour the cocktail sauce over the meat and garnish.

To prepare the cocktail sauce mix the mayonnaise and whipped cream, add ketchup, several drops of Worcester sauce, Tabasco sauce, a drop of cognac, lemon juice, salt and mix well.

Serve with buttered toast.

(1 serving amounts to 326/1369 Cal/J)

Lobster Salad

(serves 4-6)

1.6 kg. (3.5 lb.) lobster
100 ml. (4 fl. oz.) olive oil, 5 garlic cloves
parsley, salt, pepper, 1 teaspoon mustard
2 lemons, green and black olives

Cook the lobster. Cube or slice the meat. Make a mixture of the chopped garlic and parsley, salt, pepper, mustard, lemon juice and oil. Pour this mixture over the lobster pieces and fold in gently. Chill well.

Garnish the salad with lettuce leaves.

(1 serving amounts to 411/1726 Cal/J)

*L*obsters should be cooked alive. Pour water into a deep saucepan, add a little vinegar, a bay leaf,
peppercorns and salt well. When the water comes to the boil, place the lobster in it and cook for
about 30 - 45 minutes - depending on its size. When the lobster is cooked, take it out of the water, place
on a flat surface, and put a weight on it. When it cools, remove the meat from the shell and prepare
according to your recipe.

ogether with the lobster called rarog, lobsters are the largest and rarest crustaceans in the Adriatic Sea. An expensive delicacy, it is prized for its very tasty meat, which is generally prepared in a very simple way, cooked, with additions enhancing its characteristics. The best places in Croatia to find lobsters are the most distant islands, especially Vis, Lastovo, Mljet and the outer edge of the Kornati islands. Lobster is caught the whole year round, but the tastiest lobsters are the ones caught on moonlight nights.

Grilled Lobster

(serves 4-6)

2 cooked, medium-sized lobsters in their shells

50 g. (2 oz.) butter, 2 lemons

Cut the cooked and chilled lobsters longitudinally from the head to the tail. Remove the intestine with a tooth pick. Wash the inside of the head under a stream of cold wa-

Lobster Medallions
à la parisienne

(serves 4-6)

ter and dry. Brush with melted butter and place buttered side down on a well heated grill. When the lobster turns to golden brown, serve with lemon slices and with sauce, according to taste.

(1 serving amounts to 289/1214 Cal/J)

Tip:

The live lobster can be placed on the grill, but first you need to cut it into halves.

250 g. (9 oz.) cleaned lobster meat
2 tablespoons flour and 2 eggs
frying oil
salt
parsley
lemon

Slice the lobster meat into thin rounds (medallions), cover with flour. Beat the eggs

with a little salt until fluffy and dip the floured lobster pieces into this mixture before frying. Fry the lobster in medium heated oil until golden brown.

Arrange on a heated plate, garnish with lemon slices and parsley leaves.

Serve with piquant cold sauce.

(1 serving amounts to 166/697 Cal/J)

A lthough fishermen love to brag about the huge fish they
catch, especially white fish, they love small fish, too, whether white or blue. Even more so, the smallest netted

fish such as pilchards, smelts, picarels, surmullets, sea-breams, horse mackerels, milt, barely bigger then the net openings, were

prepared for the first meal on vessels or in ports at arrival. Usually the fish was only cleaned, dried, rolled in flour and fried.

After cleaning the bigger fish and cutting off their heads and taking out the backbone, they, too, were sometimes dipped in

mixed eggs and in bread crumbs, to be fried in oil. Rupice were prepared in Istria in the same manner but they were not rolled

in bread crumbs but in a mixture of wheat and corn maize flour. After frying, the excess oil was absorbed by using tissue paper.

Golden-brown, crunchy, pleasantly salted mouthfuls, served with fried potatoes, lemon slices, tomatoes or some other seasonal

salad are an excellent summer meal. Fried fish eaten from paper plates have become very popular at summer festive occasions,

and at the beach. Old seaside inhabitants consider small fish to be excellent titbits which go well with a glass of good rich

wine, because they make one even thirstier.

Fried Small Fish

Various sorts of smaller fish, such as pilchards, smelts, picarels, surmullets, seabreams, horse mackerel and others are most often prepared fried in oil.

Clean the fish, wash it and dry well. Roll in flour and fry in a well heated mixture of olive oil and sunflower oil. If necessary, lower the heat a little during frying, so that the fish becomes crunchy, but not dry.

You can also fry pilchards rolled in bread crumbs. In this case cut off their heads and remove the backbones.

Season with salt, roll in flour, then in mixed eggs and last of all in breadcrumbs. Fry them in hot oil until golden-brown.

Place the fried fish on absorbent paper and only then season with salt.

Serve with lemon slices, tomatoes or other salad of the season.

ood fish does not need complicated preparation, but only a good cook. Bigger fish, especially those with big heads, were usually boiled. Red scorpionfish were considered best for boiling. But dentex, gurnard and cod, or any other white fish is also excellent when boiled. Fishermen in the Adriatic believe that while bigger fish can be caught in the oceans, the tastiest fish are the biggish ones from a small sea.

Boiled Red Scorpionfish

(serves 4)

1.2 kg. (2.5 lb.) red scorpionfish
salt, peppercorns
1 tablespoon Vegeta, 1 bay leaf
50 g. (2 oz.) carrots
1 parsley root
1 onion
3 cloves garlic
2-3 tablespoons wine vinegar
50 g. (2 fl. oz.) olive oil, parsley

Pour water into a pan, add salt, pepper, Vegeta, a little oil, bay leaf, cleaned and diced carrots, parsley, onion and garlic. Let it boil briefly. Add vinegar, the cleaned fish and cook for about 20 minutes. Take the fish out of the soup carefully, place on an oval serving platter, arrange the boiled carrots and parsley around it. Pour a little fish soup and the rest of the oil over the fish, sprinkle with chopped parsley, and serve with boiled potatoes.

(1 serving amounts to 485/2037 Cal/J)

Tip:

Strain the soup in which the fish was cooked, add a little olive oil and tomatoes, sprinkle with pepper and serve with boiled rice.

Fish Brodetto (Soup)

(serves 4-6)

1.2 kg. (2.5 lb.) various sea fish (for instance conger eel, red scorpionfish, bonito, mackerel), 3 tablespoons flour
100 ml. (4 fl. oz.) olive oil
2 onions
5 cloves garlic
200g. (7 oz.) tomatoes or 2 tablespoons tomato puree
1-2 tablespoons wine vinegar
1 tablespoon Vegeta
salt, pepper
parsley

Clean the fish and cut into large pieces, season with salt. Roll each piece in flour. Fry briefly in hot oil on both sides. Place the fried fish on a plate. Sauté chopped onions and garlic in the remaining oil until glassy. Add the peeled tomatoes and cook some more. Return the fish to the pan, add a little vinegar, water and Vegeta. Season with more salt and pepper. Continue cooking until the fish is tender. Sprinkle with chopped parsley. Polenta is the best side dish with brodetto.

(1 serving amounts to 474/1991 Cal/J)

Note:
Do not stir the brodetto while cooking but only shake the saucepan occasionally.

Brodetto, brudet, brujet, described by the continentals as "buzara" which does not thicken due to bread crumbs but due to onion, may be prepared in many ways. Each is considered as the only authentic way. A variety of fish and vegetables can be used to make brodetto.

Cod and Potatoes

(serves 6-8)

400 g. (14 oz.) dried cod
1.5 kg. (3.5 lb.) potatoes
4 cloves garlic
250 g. (9 oz.) olive oil
bay leaf
salt
pepper
a little lemon juice or white dry wine
Vegeta
parsley

Probably the most traditional food in Dalmatia - cod - is not even an Adriatic Sea fish by origin! It was brought to Croatia on vessels from Norway, already dried in the sun. It was cheap and good food eaten by the common people, but transformed with time into a highly prized national speciality. It is most often prepared as brodetto, as a bread spread, or mixed with potatoes as a reminder of the times when people were less prosperous. It is unthinkable not to have cod on one's Christmas table or during Easter Week. But, for a long time now it has not been prepared as in the old days when it was first soaked for two days in water, then wrapped in cloth and beaten with a pounder, and then boiled for hours.

Place the soaked and softened cod in cold water to cook for about 30 minutes. Take the cod out of the stock - setting the stock aside - remove the skin and shred the fish into small pieces. Take half of the oil and

166

gently heat part of the chopped garlic. Put part of the peeled potatoes sliced thinly into irregular pieces on top. Sprinkle with Vegeta, garlic, plenty of chopped parsley. Season with pepper. Arrange a layer of cod on top, and continue until you have used up all the potatoes and cod. The last layer should be potatoes. Sprinkle with a little salt and pour in enough stock to cover all the ingredients. Add the bay leaf, the remaining oil, and cook slowly without stirring until the potatoes are cooked. Shake the saucepan occasionally during cooking. At the end add a little white wine and sprinkle with chopped parsley.

(1 serving amounts to 672/2822 Cal/J)

Eel Brodetto

(serves 4-6)

1 kg. (2 lb.) eel
100 ml. (4 fl. oz.) olive oil
200 g. (7 oz.) onion
2 small hot peppers
2 tablespoons tomato puree
about 100 ml. (4 fl. oz.) wine vinegar
salt, pepper
2 bay leaves
3 - 4 cloves garlic
parsley, 1 tablespoon Vegeta

Chop the onions finely and fry in oil until golden. Add the cleaned eel cut into slices, and the small red hot peppers. Salt a little and stew until the water evaporates. Then add tomatoes, pepper, the bay leaf, vinegar and Vegeta. Stew briefly, add a little water and leave to cook slowly. When almost ready, add chopped garlic and parsley. Do not stir during cooking, but only shake the saucepan occasionally. Polenta is the best side dish.

(1 serving amounts to 475/1995 Cal/J)

Tip:

If the eel is large, skin it, cut into pieces and fry them in oil after having rolled them in flour.

Note:

This simple brodetto is a combination of fish stew and brodetto, and is characteristic for the area around the Neretva river where the fresh river water and sea water mix. You can add frog legs to the eel, if desired.

Dentex with Potatoes

(serves 4-6)

1.2 kg. (2.5 lb.) dentex
1 kg. (2 lb.) potatoes
100 ml. (4 fl. oz.) olive and sunflower oil
1 onion
3 - 4 cloves garlic
salt, pepper, Vegeta, lemon juice
celery leaves, bay leaf, parsley

Clean the fish, and, if it is a big one, cut into pieces.
Arrange sliced potatoes in a wide pan. Put the chopped onion and garlic on top, sprinkle with salt and Vegeta. Arrange the fish sprinkled with lemon juice on top of these ingredients. Add the celeriac, the bay leaf and pour in enough water just to cover the contents of the pan. The quantity of water depends on whether you wish the dish to be thicker or soup-like. Cook over a gentle heat and shake the saucepan occasionally. When the ingredients are almost cooked, season with pepper. Serve sprinkled with chopped parsley.
(1 serving amounts to 529/2222 Cal/J)

Tip:

Other white fish can be prepared in a similar way.

Conger Eel Brijuni Style

(serves 4-6)

1.2 kg (2.5 lb.) conger eel
100 ml. (4 fl. oz.) olive oil
30 g. (1 oz.) butter
100 ml. (4 fl. oz.) white wine
parsley, lemon juice
150 g. (5 oz.) onion, 3 cloves garlic
salt, pepper
1 tablespoon capers
milk for marinade, Vegeta

Clean the fish and cut into slices. Leave to rest for about 1 hour in slightly salted milk. Take it out of the milk, drain, sprinkle with lemon drops, roll in flour and fry on both sides in a mixture of olive oil and sunflower

oil. Take the fish out of the frying pan. Fry the onion lightly in the remaining oil and then the garlic and capers. Replace the fish in the pan, sprinkle with Vegeta, season with a little salt and pepper, pour in the wine. Simmer gently about 20 minutes. Add fish stock or water occasionally. When cooked, sprinkle with chopped parsley. Serve polenta or pasta as a side dish.

In Istria *posutice* - pasta cut into small squares - would be served with this dish.

(1 serving amounts to 544/2285 Cal/J)

Tip:

You can make the fish stock by cooking the fish head and tail with soup vegetables, a bay leaf, peppercorns, a little salt and white wine about 1 hour, and then straining it.

After discovering what was edible, our forebears used plants which grew wild together with the vegetables and fruits they themselves cultivated. There is a wide variety of such plants in the Mediterranean area. Leaves and fruits are used mostly. Capers are an example of these plants, and they usually grow in rock fissures, in old walls and dry stone fences. Flower buds are picked, and preserved in wine vinegar. As time passes they develop a special aroma coming from their capric acid content. These flower buds are sometimes preserved in salted water or oil, and the smaller they are, the better they are. Sometimes they are eaten fresh. In the Dubrovnik area fruits are also preserved in vinegar. Except for garnishing, capers are also used in salads, sauces, meat and fish dishes, and in cheeses.

*oiled Swiss chard with potatoes may be served with grilled fish,
even the king of grilled fish, sea-bass. This seemingly modest dish
may turn out to be quite a surprise. Boil the Swiss chard in a small quantity
of water. You can alter the potato quantity and the way it is cut - into cubes
or slices. You can also mash the potatoes together with the Swiss chard.*

*Various cabbage-like vegetables can be added to this mixture, even wild
growing green leafy vegetables to be more like the popular mišanca (mixture). This mixture varies from settlement to settlement, but the seasoning is
the same everywhere: olive oil, garlic, fresh parsley, salt, pepper, Vegeta ...*

Grilled
Sea-Bass

(serves 4-6)

| 1 sea-bass (about 1.2 kg./2.5 lb.) |
| 100 ml. (4 fl. oz.) olive oil |
| parsley, salt, pepper |
| rosemary, bay leaf, lemon juice |

Dry the cleaned sea-bass, salt and put
chopped parsley, pepper, rosemary, the bay
leaf and a little lemon juice inside it. Place
the fish on a hot grill and cook gently on
both sides. Baste with oil occasionally. If you
do not have a grill, you can bake the fish in
the oven.

(1 serving amounts to 373/1567 Cal/J)

Roast Gilthead in Wine

(serves 4-6)

1.5 kg. (4 lb.) gilthead
salt, freshly ground pepper
1.5 kg. (4 lb.) potatoes
150 ml. (5 fl. oz.) olive oil
200 ml. (8 fl. oz.) white wine
parsley
3 cloves garlic
rosemary
bay leaf
lemon juice
Vegeta

Clean the gilthead and dry outside and inside with absorbent paper. Before cooking cut it slightly and sprinkle with a little salt and pepper.

Cut the potatoes into slices, season with a little salt, add oil, making sure the potato slices are well covered with it. Place in a baking tin, arrange the prepared fish on top and put in a heated oven to bake for about 50 minutes at 200°C/400°F/Gas Mark 6.

Baste with oil occasionally.

In the meantime prepare a mixture combining wine, a little water or fish stock, oil, chopped parsley, garlic, rosemary, bay leaf, lemon juice, a little salt, pepper and Vegeta. When the fish is almost cooked pour the prepared mixture over it.

The gilthead and potatoes can be served in the tin they were baked in.

(1 serving amounts to 757/3179 Cal/J)

A grill is not just any barbecue. It is very important how you build the a fire. It is best to use dry vine and spruce with a pine needle or so. No less important are rosemary and bay twigs soaked in olive oil, used for basting fish. Whether cut into thick slices or broiled whole, a fish is considered well done if it is juicy, cooked near the bone too, but not falling apart. Even frozen fish are considered good, but they must be of good quality and defrosted before they are grilled. In the past it was a rule to cook white fish and to fry blue fish, but nowadays it does not have to be so. On the other hand, it is still the ritual to serve grilled fish with only a small bowl of olive oil, seasoned with chopped garlic and fresh parsley. There is nothing else to it, but to carefully choose the fish and wood for the fire, and enjoy yourself until the grilled fish and the wine are on the table.

Grilled Bonito

(serves 4)

1 kg. (2 lb.) bonito or tuna
150 ml. (5 fl. oz.) olive oil, 4 cloves garlic
bay leaf, pepper, salt, lemon, parsley
rosemary twig, Vegeta

Dry the cleaned fish and cut into even slices. Arrange the slices in a pan and pour in a mixture of 100 ml. (4 fl. oz.) oil, 2 crushed garlic cloves, pepper, bay leaf and Vegeta. Let the fish rest for two hours and then grill it gentlyl for about 15 minutes, first on one side and then on the other. Baste the fish with the rosemary twig soaked in oil. Arrange the cooked fish on a plate, garnish with lemon and parsley. Serve with baked eggplant and zucchini salad seasoned with pepper, slices of garlic, vinegar and olive oil.
(1 serving amounts to 393/1651 Cal/J)

Grilled Mackerel

(serves 4)

1 kg. (2 lb.) mackerel
100 ml. (4 fl. oz.) olive oil and sunflower oil mixture
salt
parsley
lemon

Wash the cleaned fish, dry and season with salt. Place on a well heated grill. Baste continuously with a rosemary twig soaked in oil. Arrange the cooked mackerel on a plate and garnish with lemon and parsley. The fish can be served with grilled tomato slices.

(1 serving amounts to 417/1751 Cal/J)

Note:

You can prepare other sorts of blue fish in the same manner (bonito, tuna, pilchards, horse mackerel).

Tip:

If you are using frozen fish it is best to marinade it first in a mixture of olive oil, crushed garlic, bay leaf, rosemary, pepper and salt. Cover the defrosted, well dried mackerel with marinade and leave to rest about 2 hours before grilling.

Fritters

*C*hristmas would not be Christmas without fritters, loved by all Mediterranean coastal inhabitants. Whatever form they take, they are always made from risen dough fried in oil. Brandy is added so that they do not absorb too much fat. Today they are prepared in a more simple way, often yoghurt-based, or with baking powder. Our recipe is a more sophisticated variant of potato based fritters. But wherever fritters are made - in Dalmatia, Istria or Dalmatinska Zagora - they will be tastier and better if a large number of eggs is used, and crispy proportionally to the number of fine ingredients added.

500 g. (1 lb.) white potatoes
200 g. (7 oz.) flour
1 sachet instant dry yeast
2 eggs, 40 g. (1.5 oz.) sugar
50 ml. (2 fl. oz.) rum, a little brandy
50 g. (2 oz.) sultanas or raisins
lemon and orange peel
nutmeg
vanilla sugar
oil for frying
caster sugar for dredging

Wash the potatoes, boil and peel while still hot, and put through a potato press. Mix the mashed, slightly cooled potatoes with beaten eggs, sugar, rum, grated lemon and orange peel, brandy, grated nutmeg and vanilla sugar. Blend well and add the flour mixed with dry yeast, sultanas or raisins soaked in rum. Add a pinch of salt and mix again adding a little lukewarm water so that the dough has a medium-thick texture. Beat the dough with a wooden spoon until it becomes smooth and glossy. Leave in a warm place to prove for about 1 hour.

Heat a generous quantity of oil, and keep it at boiling point during frying. Dip a spoon into the oil so that the dough does not stick, take a spoonful of dough and drop it into the boiling oil. Fry the fritters until golden brown. Do not put too many fritters into the oil at once because you must turn them during frying.

Serve hot, sprinkled with caster sugar.

(1 serving amounts to 331/1390 Cal/J)

Tip:
You can form fritters with your hands: take some dough into your hand, squeeze the dough between the thumb and forefinger, spoon off the dough that comes out (the size of a walnut), drop it into boiling oil and fry.

Fruit Tart

250 g. (9 oz.) flour
150 g. (5 oz.) butter
70 g. (2 1/3 oz.) sugar
40 g. (1.5 oz.) almonds
lemon rind
2 egg yolks
Vanilla cream:
3 egg yolks
3 tablespoons sugar
10 g. (1/2 oz.) cornflour
1 sachet vanilla sugar
250 ml. (12 fl. oz.) milk
rum
Jelly and Fruit Topping:
400 g. (14 oz.) fresh fruit (peaches, kiwi,
berries, or compote fruit)
1 tablespoon caster sugar
1 packet "Dr. Oetker" Tart Jelly

Crumb well the flour with butter cut into flakes, add sugar, egg yolks, ground almonds, grated lemon rind, and make a shortcrust dough. Leave to rest in a cool place for about 1 - 2 hours.

Knead the dough a little and roll out into a round, the size of a shallow tart pan. Butter the pan and spread dough over the pan, raising the dough a little at the sides. Bake for about 20 minutes at 200°C/400°F/Gas Mark 6.

Cool the baked tart and spread with a layer of vanilla cream. Arrange washed and well drained fruit on top, sprinkle with caster sugar. Prepare the jelly according to instructions, pour over the fruit and chill. Serve the tart with whipped cream.

To prepare the vanilla cream mix the egg yolks and sugar well, add vanilla sugar, cornflour and a little cold milk. Mix well and cook in the remaining hot milk. Cook for about 8 - 10 minutes at a moderate temperature until it thickens. Add rum to taste. Chill the cream.

(1 serving amounts to 212/890 Cal/J)

Fritters - Kroštule

200 g. (7 oz.) flour, 3 egg yolks
1 tablespoon sugar, 2 tablespoons rum, 1
tablespoon sour cream, salt
caster sugar for sprinkling, frying oil

Sift the flour. Whisk the eggs until fluffy. Add the whisked eggs, salt, sugar, sour cream and rum to the flour and knead into a firm dough. Leave to rest for about half an hour, roll out thinly. Cut into strips using a fluted pastry-cutting wheel. Shape the strips as you like and fry them in deep hot oil. Place the fried kroštule on absorbent paper tissue. Arrange them on a plate and sprinkle with a mixture of caster sugar and vanilla sugar.

(1 serving amounts to 301/1268 Cal/J)

*T*he continental doughnut has long become an everyday sweet in other European countries as well, but Mediterranean Croatia still treasures kroštule for crazy Carnival time. They are a welcome treat served with grape brandy, when friends come together. Doughnuts have become so popular that they have replaced almost completely other variants of fried leavened dough. Sometimes the very refreshing cakes have the aroma and tastiness of Mediterranean fruit.

Pinca

1 kg. (2 lb.) flour
2 sachets dried instant yeast
200 g. (7 oz.) butter, 200 g. (7 oz.) sugar
1 sachet vanilla sugar
3 egg yolks, 400 ml. (16 fl. oz.) milk
lemon and orange rind
a dot of rum, a dot of brandy, salt
For coating:
1 egg and coarsely crushed sugar

*I*n Dalmatia there is a traditional cake for each holiday. Easter can not be without the Easter Cake - pinca, pinica, sirnica. This hard cake prepared from a large number of eggs is symbolic of Lent - restrained and lean. Together with decorated eggs it is taken to the church for blessing in the Easter basket. Afterwards it is served at the holiday breakfast, usually with ham.

Mix the yeast and flour. Leave the butter to soften and mix into the flour. Add sugar, egg yolks, vanilla sugar, grated lemon and orange rind, rum, brandy and a little salt. Make a firm dough, adding lukewarm milk when necessary. Knead until it is of smooth consistency. It should be firmer than any other leavened dough. Leave to prove in a warm place until it doubles in size. Divide the dough into 3 - 4 pieces, and form into a ball (pinca). Place each ball separately on greased paper and allow to rise again. When they have risen well, make three deep equidistant cuts on the pinca tops in three directions. Brush with fluffily beaten egg and sprinkle with coarsely crushed sugar. Bake for about for 30 - 40 minutes in the oven at 200°C/400°F/Gas Mark 6.

(1 serving amounts to 330/1386 Cal/J)

"Maraska" Paradiso

(serves 6)

5 - 6 eggs, 150 g. (5 oz.) sugar
1 tablespoon cornflour
1 l. (1.75 pints) milk
vanilla bean or vanilla sugar
Sour cherry sauce:
250 g. (9 oz.) stewed sour cherries
(strained and pitted)
100 ml. (4 fl. oz.) liquid in which the sour
cherries were stewed
1 teaspoon caster sugar
1 teaspoon cornflour

a little maraschino liqueur
chopped roasted almonds

Mix the egg yolks and sugar until fluffy and add cornflour. Beat the egg whites to the stiff peak stage adding 1 tablespoon sugar taken from the measured quantity. Place the vanilla bean into the milk and bring to the boil. Remove the milk from the heat, and place spoonfuls of the beaten egg whites into the pan. Return to the stove, but only until the milk begins to boil. Turn over the snow balls. After a couple of seconds re-move them from the pan and place in a deep bowl. Repeat until all the snow balls are cooked.

Pour the boiling milk left over from cook-ing over the mixed egg yolks, mix well and place the pan over the heat again. Let it boil briefly, stirring continuously.

Pour the hot sauce over the snow balls, add the sour cherry sauce, and sprinkle with chopped roasted almonds.

(1 serving amounts to: 285/1197 Cal/J)

Sour cherry sauce:

Boil briefly the sour cherries, part of the stewed cherries liquid, maraschino and caster sugar. Add cornflour previously mixed with the remaining juice. Boil briefly until the sauce becomes thick.

Rožata

*1 litre (1.75 pints) milk, 300 g. (11 oz.)
granulated sugar
a little lemon rind, 7 eggs, 2 egg yolks
100 g. (4 oz.) granulated sugar for caramel
butter to coat the moulds*

Put the milk, sugar, vanilla sugar, and a little lemon rind to cook in a saucepan. Cool. Beat the eggs and egg yolks. Mix with the milk. Pour the mixture into a big mould, or smaller moulds, as desired. Before doing this, butter the moulds and coat with caramel. Bake in the oven for about 40 minutes at 220°C/425°F/Gas Mark 7, or for 20 minutes if the moulds are small. When half-way done, place the moulds in a water bath and continue to bake. Rožata may also be cooked over steam, covered.

(1 serving amounts to 339/1424 Cal/J)

Caramel:

Put the sugar in a saucepan with a little water and allow to caramelize until golden brown.

Sweets are not a favourite with Adriatic Coast inhabitants. This lack of taste for sweets was not caused by the lack of a wide variety of fresh fruits - sour cherries, figs, oranges. Due to the hot climate, food could not be kept long. Two traditional Dalmatian sweets uncover the doubtless connections with other world countries from which interesting recipes and extracts and foodstuffs arrived. The paradise desert "Maraska" is the classical recipe for snowballs which are well loved in the north too, but in Dalmatia they are additionally flavoured with the best sour cherries in the world, the Dalmatian maraska and maraska liqueur, and also with almonds. Cream prepared from a large quantity of eggs topped with caramel is a favourite in international cuisine. Dubrovnik inhabitants proclaim their rožata as something completely different. But this is the case with all the rest, all the way to the north Adriatic towns. They are all so enthusiastic that they even find proof of exclusivity in the stone rosettas of their palaces and churches. The cooks from the past could remind them of several rose oil drops which were used as flavouring and which gave the original aroma to the various types of this popular sweet.

CROATIAN WINES

A piece of land snatched away from the Karst and made into terraced vineyards on the hills surrounding the town of Primošten is a painting motif worthy to decorate the United Nations building in New York. But these could just as well have been the vineyard terraces above Bakar, from the island of Korčula, or the continental Kutjevo or Ilok vineyards. Croatia can boast of the rare wealth concentrated in its vine-growing hills and its wines, ranging "from northern fine white wines to southern red wines". Not many things have as lengthy a history as wines do, and in Croatia, the Korčula white wine "Grk", for instance, judging from the Lumbarda archaeological findings, has its roots in the vine cultivated in the Hellenic period. The Hvar and Vis coins which have imprinted grapes and pitchers on them date from the 4th century B.C., as well as glasses and jugs. Two centuries later the Greek writer Athenaios quotes the words of Agataride from the island of Knidos, which say that the best wine is produced on the island of Vis. In our times Mate Balota wrote the song called "Kalavojna" (good wine) telling of the Istrian legend about the Argonauts and vineyard planting.

Vines are known to have been cultivated in the area of present-day Croatia for more than six thousand years, while viniculture expanded especially from Roman times. The Romans comprehended that vines have very well developed roots and could prosper in places where other plants do not have a chance of survival. So vines were planted everywhere, on hilly areas, sloping land, whether sandy or poor, or dry. An ancient grape press was discovered in Istria, in the place called Barbariga near Fažana, and in Rovinjsko selo, and there is a temple in the vicinity of Poreč dedicated to the wine god Bacchus with a grave monument depicting two vines and a grape-harvester picking grapes and putting them in a basket. The name of the town Novi Vinodol is a direct translation of the Roman name. Emperor Claudius had Moslavačka gora in northern Croatia planted with vines in the 1st century, and this is where the name Mons Claudius comes from. Dating from the Emperor Domician, wines had to be protected with various protective measures from the Pannonian wines, and these measures were also brought by emperors to follow. They were annulled only by Emperor Probo, an Illyrian, in the 3rd century, and thus vine-growing developed again in Baranja, in Slavonija around Požega, and in Hrvatsko Zagorje around Krapina, Vinagora, Lobor, Petrijanec. It seemed that the great migrations would lead to destruction of the vineyards, but vine-growing spread with the

spread of Christianity, due to the fact that wine is also a part of church rituals. On arrival in their new homeland, the Croats would adopt viniculture and wine production. Grapevines and wine are mentioned in many historical documents ("Listina Rižanskog sabora" from 804. "Istarski razvod", "Vinodolski zakonik" from 1288). The "Korčulanski statut" of 1407 shows how important this branch of agriculture was, threatening that a lessee of land would lose all the vineyard income if he did not perform all the necessary work in tending it. Those intentionally damaging vineyards would have their right hand cut off, and if the guilty person was not found in two weeks, the whole settlement had to pay for the damage. The Dubrovnik Statute regulates conscientious vineyard cleaning: the first hoeing had to be done by the middle of March, and the second by the day of St. Vitus. The importance of wine production may be seen in the complaints made by the town of Split to the Venetian Doge concerning wine imports from other regions. The inhabitants of Split

"had no other revenues except those from wine production, and all inhabitants were living on this alone". In this century, Mate Balota described the food of Croats on Venetian galleys up to the middle of the last century as traditionally consisting of two meals, breakfast at seven and dinner at two. "There were salted pilchards with oil for breakfast with vinegar, bread and wine", and wine was also distributed at dinner.

Wine production was also very important in the continental part of present-day Croatia. On the near-by Zagrebačka Gora were the vineyards of the ecclesiastic Kaptol and the nobles. The first written document from this area dates from 1209 when Andrija II granted the town of Varaždin the rights of a free town and obliged it to give 20 bucketsful of wine to the Varaždin castle district-perfect. But this was probably not an onerous duty as Varaždin-Breg is still famous for its vineyards. The Golden Bull dating from 1220, the document on the foundation of Zagreb, mentions the Medvednica vineyards. The Cistercians, founded in 1232, cultivated the vine-

yards of Kutjevo and took care of the cellars until they came under Turkish control in 1529. After their withdrawal, the vineyards were cultivated by the Jesuits. The Đakovo bishopry cultivates vineyards on Mandićevac and Trnava, Prince Eugen of Savoy in Baranja, the Odescalch counts in the Ilok area, the counts Eltz on the Vukovar landed estate, and the Čeh family in Erdut. The very well known cellars and vineyards of the eastern Slavonian Danube Basin, damaged in the recent war, will surely be revitalised, and the pre-war archive wines, like the Ilok Graševina restored to its former glory and again win prizes for its quality.

The tax reformation in 1753 paid special attention to vineyards because they covered a significant part of land area, although systematic viniculture reformation began only in 1841 when the society equivalent to today's Chamber of Commerce ordered that 50,000 vine-shoots should be procured, based on the proposal of the town wine-grower, Trummer. Since then there has been a saying that wealth and glory lie in wine. After 1864, when vines began to be grafted in Europe, wine became Croatia's most important product. Barely ten years afterwards, Croatian wines are awarded prizes at the world wine exhibitions held in London and Vienna. At the end of the 19th century vine-pest was transferred to Europe from America. Together with oidium and peronospora it completely destroyed the old vineyards at their roots by the turn of the nineteenth to the twentieth century. Many vine-growers left their homeland and, today, Croatian wine-growers such as Grgich are well-known from California to New Zealand. Vine-growing in Croatia was revived with difficulty, based on new, American shoots resistant to vine-pest. After a long period of regression, viniculture was restored in Croatia, particularly after World War II. At the world competition in France in 1996, the best Chardonnay was proclaimed as the one produced by the Tomac family from Jaska.

White sorts are grown all over the continental Croatian area: Graševina, Rhenish Riesling, Traminac, Green Silvanac, Sauvignon, White and Grey Burgundac, Muškat Ottonel, Moslavac, as well as red sorts: Frankovka, Burgundac, Cabernet Sauvignon and Cab-

ernet Franc, etc. White sorts like Kraljevina, Škrlet, Štajerska Belina and Veltlinac, and red Kavčina and Portugizac are grown in the west regions only, and white Rizvanac, red Merlot and Kadarka in the east regions only. The assortment in the coastal region is much wider. White sorts are grown in Istria and the Littoral region : Malvazija, Burgundac, Trbljan, Opačevina, Žlahtina, Gegić, red Borgonja, Teran, Merlot, Barbera, Cabernet Sauvignon and Cabernet Franc, Hrvatica, Plavina, red Muškat. The following white sorts are grown in north Dalmatia and Dalmatinska Zagora: Debit, Trbljan, Maraština, Gegić, Kujundžuša, Zlatarica and Žilavka. Žilavka is also called Mostarska Žilavka because this old Herzegovinian sort is grown all the way from Mostar to Metković and Imotski. Although grown mainly on rocky land, its grapes are made into a wine which is light yellow-green in colour, and

has a pleasant aroma and strong taste. Red sorts grown in these regions are : Plavina, Galica, Zadarka, Babić, Lasina, Ninčuša, Okatac, Rudežuša, Blatina, Trnjak... Maraština, Trbljan, Zlatarica, Bogdanuša, Vugava, Kurtelaška, Cetinka, Pošip, Grk, Malvasija Dubrovačka, are the white sorts grown in the central and southern Dalmatian regions, and Plavac Mali, Plavac Veliki, Okatac, Vranac, Kadarun, Dobričić Plavina, Babić, Ninčuša the red sorts. Kardinal, Julski Muškat, Kraljica Vinograda, Alphonse Lavalee, Muškat Hamburg, Afus-ali are the table grapes most often grown in those regions. Outside the wine-growing hills, old sorts and new hybrids are grown in lower continental areas.

In the last decade much has been done in connection with the improvement of vine-growing and wine-making methods, and in respect to the maintenance of geographical protected wine-growing areas, and there is an increasing number of good wine-shops.

The first protected Croatian wine was Dingač 1961, made from the Plavac Mali sort, and it was soon joined by other protected wines, such as: Postup-Potomje, Postup-Donja Banda from Pelješac, and Pošip-Čara-Smokvica and Maraštin-Čara-Smokvica from the island of Korčula. Of the 697 wines with controlled geographical origin protected to date, 76 sorts may be considered as élite ones. These are some of them: Bujska Malvazija, Hrvatica HI Agrieno Umag, Porečki Muškat Ottonel, Porečki Cabernet Sauvignon and Porečki Merlot Agrolagune Poreč, Buzetski Teran Agroprodukta Buzet, Vrbnička Žlahtina PZ Vrbnik, Primoštenski Babić Vinoploda Šibenik, Viška Vugava PZ Podšpilje, Bolski Plavac PZ Bol, Faros from the Starigrad wine-cellar, Plavac Ivan Dolac PZ Svirče, Zla-

tan Plavac "Vitisa" from Jelsa, Bogdanuša Plančić, Mimićki Plavac PZ Mimice.

Postup Donja Banda PZ Postup and Dingač PZ Potomje are the well-known red wines from the Pelješac penninsula, and Pošip is the famous white wine from the island of Korčula. Some additional well-known wines are Lumardski Grk PZ Lumbarda, Branimirov Grk produced by Branimir Cebalo, Lastovska Maraština PZ Lastovo (Lastovo Island), Dubrovačka Malvasija "Dubrovkinje", red Portugizac produced by Drago Režek from the Plešivica hillside vineyards, Rizling Rajnski produced by Željko Jambrović from Jastrebarsko, Chardonnay produced by Zdravko Tomc and Silvanac Zeleni produced by Slavko Bolt, Rajnski Rizling from Štrigova, Sauvignon by PD Čakovec, Sauvignon produced by Franjo Lebar, Žuti Muskat produced by Milan Židov, Chardonnay from Urban and Muškat Ottonel produced by Stjepan Matanović, "Šem-pjen" by Ivan Turk, Rajnski Rizling and Pinot Sivi produced by the St. Jakob wine-cellar from Božjakovina, Pinot Bijeli Svetoivanski by Stjepan Jarec from Sveti Ivan Zelina, Rajnski Rizling produced by Mirko Kos from Hrnjanac, Moslavački Pinot Bijeli and Moslavački Škrlet produced by Moslavačko Vinogorje Voloder, white wines: Kutjevačka Graševina, Chardonnay, Kutjevački Rajnski Rizling and wines by PPK Kutjevo, Rajnski Rizling and Graševina produced by Ivan Enjingi, Graševina by Vlado Krauthaker, Traminac Zeleni and the red wine Frankovka PP Orahovica, white: Rizling Rajnski, Iločki Traminac and Chardonnay VUPIK Vukovar, Graševina Pajzoš LŠG "Jelen" Ilok, Erdutska Graševina, Traminac Mirisavi and Erdustki Pinot Bijeli IPK Osijek Erdut, Beljski Rizling and Beljski Pinot Bijeli PIK Belje Kneževi Vinogradi, Graševina "Dolci" by Marija Zdjelarević Aničić from Brodski Stupnik, Trnavački Traminac from Biskupija Đakovo, Mandićevačka graševina and Mandićevački Pinot Bijeli produced by PIK Đakovo.

Vine-yards, grapes and wine were always highly respected by the Croats, and traces of this respect in the Croatian heritage may be found in the form of embroidered folk costumes, customs and sayings, in literature, paintings and sculptures, architecture, theatre and motion pictures. As is the

case with other peoples, wine is connected with health and illness, joy and grief. Due to its antiviral and antibacterial properties, wine was considered to have magic powers. In their book *100 Croatian Wines* Ivica Medved and Marijan Ričković mention Bikla, the old Croatian drink with healing properties (Smutica, Zdravljak, Poluša), which is an equal mixture of uncooked milk (goats milk primarily) and wine, and is still consumed today in the Dalmatinska zagora region and on some islands. The Istrian "soup" is also considered as a beverage giving energy, and is consumed when the heaviest work is being done.

Wine is so highly respected that it is mentioned even in the national anthem. There are many popular drinking songs. All the work and doings connected with wine and vine-growing are found in old customs. January 22 is *Vincekovo*, the vine celebration day when grape-vines are "watered" with wine and bestowed with food, sausages for instance,

and the future harvesting is called for by the first cut off branching grape-vine. Grape-gathering is a very special occasion, as well as *Martinje* on November 11 when unfermented grape juice turns to wine, and is served with roast goose and chestnuts. There is a custom linked with this date called *Križevački štatuti*, organised today mainly for tourists.

Such wine parties are organised by wine clubs of vine-growing regions, ranging from the towns of Varaždin, Krapina, Križevci, Sisak, Petrinja, Karlovac, Ivanić-Grad, Bjelovar, Koprivnica, Đurđevac, Samobor, Požega to Zagreb and Vinkovci, all in accordance with the "regule" (rules on wine consuming), following the Wine Experts Society called "Pinta", founded in 1696 near the town of Varaždin by the great admirer of fine wine, Baron Baltazar Patačić, and his friends who were capable of drinking a "pinut" full of wine. In *Gazophylacium* published in 1740 the writer, Belostenec, gives many characteristics of wine. A very special occasion at table is combining the dish-es and beverages. No matter how strictly the basic principles are followed: from the lighter to the heavier,

from the lighter in colour to the darker, from the colder to the less cold, there is one general conclusion - Croatian dishes go best with Croatian wines. If we follow the recommendations of Nevenko Fazlić and Vinko Milat in the book *Croatian Wines*, dry strong white wine (Porečka Malvazija Slatka or Prošek) will be served as aperitifs. Fermented strong white wines, aromatic with a full bouquet are usually served with soup (Traminac Mirisavi, Burgundac Bijeli, Rizling Rajnski, Malvazija). If the hors-d'ouevres are shellfish or crabs, light neutral wines are recommended (Vrbnička Žlahtina, Plešivička Kraljevina, Štrigovanec), and if the cold hors d'oeuvres are prosciutto (Parma ham), ham, sausages, goose liver, pate and the like, dry white wines, or light red ones are served (such as Varaždinec, Debit Promina, Benkovački Rose, Kujundžuša). With egg and meat hors d'oeuvres, or pasta with meat sauce, light red wines go well (Moslavačka Frankovka, Šiler, Hrvatica). Aged white wine (Erdutska Graševina, Đakovački Rizling,

Međimurska Graševina, Porečki Pinot Bijeli) go best with white boiled fish, or boiled light meat with horseradish. If the main dish is grilled, fried or baked fish or fish brodetto (soup), the best choice is medium strong red wine (Motovunski Teran, Zadarski Grenche, Kaštelet Crni). White dry wines (Moslavac, Škrlet, Klikun Bijeli, Kaštelet Bijeli, Cetinka) go well with light roasts and chicken, and red medium strong wine (Kutjevački Burgundac Crni, Maestoso, Frankovka Crna, Merlot Crni) with game or strong, heavy red wine (Porečki Cabernet Sauvignon, Primoštenski Babić, Faros, Bolski Plavac) with wild game - poultry. Aged red wines (Ilочка Frankovka Crna, Porečki Barrique 85, Postup) are a fine accompaniment to cheese, and semi-dry and sweet red and white wines (Dingač, Grk, Porečki Muškat Crveni) with sweets. Dessert wines (Malvasija Slatka, Muškat Ottonel, semi-dry champagne) compliment fruits. Coffee may be served with liqouers, Cognac, and Brandy (Maraschino, Cherry, "Glembaj"). Cheers!

CONTENTS - RECIPES IN ALPHABETICAL ORDER

CONTENTS